Hope

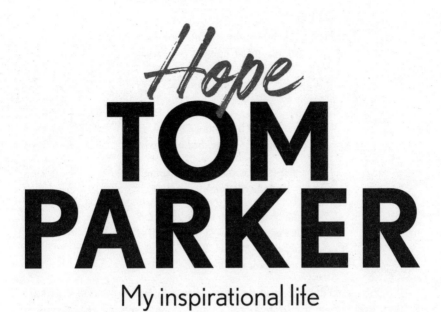

Hope

TOM PARKER

My inspirational life

BLINK
bringing you closer

With thanks to Grant Brydon

First published in the UK by Blink Publishing
An imprint of Bonnier Books UK
4th Floor, Victoria House,
Bloomsbury Square,
London, WC1B 4DA

Owned by Bonnier Books
Sveavägen 56, Stockholm, Sweden

facebook.com/blinkpublishing
twitter.com/blinkpublishing

Hardback – 978-1-788-707-16-9
Trade Paperback – 978-1-788-707-17-6
Ebook – 978-1-788-707-18-3
Audiobook – 978-1-788-707-19-0

A CIP catalogue of this book is available from the British Library.

Designed by Envy Design Ltd
Printed and bound in Great Britain by Clays Ltd, Elcograf S.p.A.

1 3 5 7 9 10 8 6 4 2

Blink Publishing is an imprint of Bonnier Books UK
www.bonnierbooks.co.uk

Say my name like it's the last time, live today like it's your last night.

We want to cry but we know it's alright, because I'm with you and you're with me, butterflies, butterflies, we were meant to fly.

In Loving Memory
of Tom Parker

Tom, I miss you so much. I don't know where you are now, but I am so honoured we got to spend time together on earth.

An honour.

I keep reminding myself to be grateful for that time, and I really, really am. I am.

You knew how to live life, fearlessly and with heart. You were so reassuring to be around. What a man. I can't believe that it's all memories now. Every single memory now is priceless. Life is a gift and you made use of yours in the most powerful ways: you made your dreams come true, you found the love of your life, you brought two beautiful humans down to earth, you sang so, so powerfully, and beautifully, and that will never die.

Everyone remembers the day they met you. You didn't slip into anyone's life quietly, you hit them like a ton of bricks and looked them square in the eyes. You talked to absolutely everyone as if they were no more and no less than you. What a man. You really took your place in the world and you are so loved. I just wish you had more time, that's selfish. You did amazing things. I just miss you. Thank you for always being there for me, without fail, always turning up, always looking out, always setting me straight lol. Okay, enough. Give 'em Hell.

I love you forever. From JayBird.

@birdspotting

Tom, my brother, my boy, my band mate, my best bud. You lit up so many lives all over the world but I can only speak on behalf of mine.

From the minute I met you, I knew this was gonna be a special chapter in my life. I was right. We did everything together, some amazing things, some outrageous things. I'm so proud of what we achieved as band mates and as brothers. I'm also proud that I was there the night you met Kels. I remember saying to you, 'You like her, don't you?'... To which you replied, 'Bro, like you wouldn't believe'. You two really are like peas and carrots.

Thank you for choosing me as your friend. It was an honour from day one. I'm so grateful I was with you until the very end. The courage and dignity I have witnessed over the last few months surpassed the lion I already knew you were.

The huge hole now left in my life will forever be there, but I know your spirit will live on through your two beautiful babies, your wonderful wife, our music, your fans, and in my heart.

I'm heartbroken beyond words right now and I cannot even begin to imagine what the future holds without you, but whatever I do going forward, even on my darkest days, I can always smile and say, 'I shared the stage with Tom Parker'.

I am going to miss you so much. I love you mate. Always. George

@MaxGeorge

Hey Tom, I hope you're having a blast up there. I am so grateful that I had a chance to witness your true courage. It has been an absolute pleasure, Tommy Boy. Thank you for letting us see you light up the world. Talk to you soon and see you later. Love you brother x

@SivaOfficial

Tom was the most passionate, funny, driven and inspiring person you could wish to meet, and I'm so grateful that I was given the honour of being a part of his journey, and even more grateful I can call him my friend as well as one of four brothers. He was the reason that the band came back together and the last six months have been the greatest pleasure of my life. Our lives will never be the same... Thank you Tom for bringing your light to the world. I hope we meet again one day, rest well, brother.

@NathanSykes

CONTENTS

Part Two

FOREWORD

BY NOREEN PARKER

As parents, we hope that our children reach and achieve all they are capable of, realising their hopes and dreams and in some respects, a tiny bit of ours; the threads of those dreams and hopes layered into the very fabric of their being.

We strived for our two boys to have the philosophy that anything is possible with the right knowledge, self-belief and application – all the things that we, as parents, initially had to scramble for as we progressed as a family.

Tom was the epitome of that optimism, coming into the world on 4 August 1988 in a hurry: a two-hour labour and there he was. He was placed in one of those plastic cribs, where he promptly raised himself up on his arms to have a good nosey around the room. The elderly nurse had to quickly rush over to him as his head was nearly over the edge! The sides of the crib were quite deep, so this was no mean feat for a newborn. I remember her words, 'Well, it looks like this one's been here before.' Those words resonated with me because they felt as if they rang true; as if he couldn't wait to get started, no time to hang around. He stayed awake for most of his first day on Earth, much to the amusement of everyone on the ward. And the die was cast: he wasn't going to miss anything, ever! He was the same since – never wanting to miss anything, alert and aware of everything around him.

Tom was a happy baby with lots of energy, always wanting to play and be entertained. He walked at ten months old (in an era when it was frowned upon to allow babies to walk before a year old as this would surely cause bandy legs) but there was no stopping him. He was off and that was that – and with no bandy legs! His speech development was the very same – he learned to speak so quickly and started to sing almost alongside his speaking, humming songs in perfect tune (unlike his tone-deaf mother!). His tuneful voice was most definitely passed down from his dad, who was a great singer. He adored travelling in the car, listening to the radio and my music tapes. (Is it child cruelty to force your little ones to listen to Genesis, Motown, rock music and Northern Soul?) He sang his heart out to all of them and knew every word and beat at five years old, much to the annoyance of his older brother Lewis, who preferred a more sedentary drive to school. In fact, the only thing to mar this perfect picture was my vocal input and even at that tender young age, Tom would say, 'Mum, don't sing, please!'

His first public performance was as an angel in the school nativity play – he was such a tiny tot that he had to be stood on a high plinth so that the audience could see him. In contrast, the strength of his voice for such a small person made everyone gasp and they couldn't believe how well he sang. I was in tears to hear him sing like the angel he was dressed as, but with a slightly gravelly voice!

As he grew, Tom developed many passions, football and gymnastics being just a couple and the whole family followed Bolton Wanderers F.C. He loved to go to the matches with his dad and played in a local team, Dad faithfully taking him weekly, no matter what the weather. He excelled in all the things he was interested in, not so much the ones he wasn't! He had an amazing talent for observation (harking back to his nosiness). This highly tuned observational skill allowed him to watch others and copy them in the minutest of detail, which was fantastic for his gymnastics but not so good for his football – observing a young Ronaldo who, at that time, after a tackle, liked to roll along the football pitch as if he'd been shot. Tom thought he would copy this to the letter and so developed the skill to a fine art. In fact, he could have also been an excellent actor, should he have chosen that path; the only person that I have ever known that could lie and convince you that he wasn't, to the point of moving himself to tears and finally believing that he was actually telling the truth.

As he grew, his natural positivity ensured that he treated every person with respect and equality and remained grounded throughout the rapid rise of suddenly being hurled into the world of pop and celebrity status with The Wanted. As parents, we had concerns as to how he would manage the dizzy heights of fame and success. The testament to his personality, however, came to the fore not during their fame, but when the band ended abruptly. After four years of riding on the crest of a wave, they were suddenly plunged into the abyss – no phasing out, just that's it, finished. Tom, nevertheless, had the usual philosophy that as one door closes, another opens and so he began the process of teaching himself how to produce, leading to a new adventure with Ollie Marland and Lost + Found. It took time, longer than Tom's patience would allow, and the uncertainty made it difficult at times, but with belief in himself and the project and his ever-present positive stance, they became successful. It is that resilience that makes us proud of him, the belief that there is always a different route to be sought out if you can think outside of the box and realise that roadblocks can be dismantled.

This approach was even more significant during his most recent journey, the toughest of his life. After the initial shock following a brain tumour diagnosis, Tom automatically went into 'Let's find a solution' mode and started to research different routes, never just accepting the standard approach and highlighting the need for more research and funding. He bravely went onto media channels to raise awareness of the lack of funding and was laid bare in his documentary for Stand Up to Cancer UK, *Inside My Head* (2021) to show that his cancer journey was just as devastating as every other person's. His natural ability, however, to remain positive and optimistic throughout the situation shone through and he inspired many others going through the same circumstance.

Our children learn so much from us, but we, in turn, learn so much from them (navigating the world of technology being one example!). Perhaps adopting their courage and confidence to create new possibilities without the fear of failure is an overriding feature.

As a family, we have been through so many situations with Tom, good and bad, and we have nothing but love and pride not only for his achievements, but also his positive attitude, resourcefulness and determination. We will always see him riding the crest of a wave (just different waves) and will always be faithfully and unswervingly at his side.

He was an amazing son and brother, whom we love dearly.

Noreen Parker, March 2022

Part One

'Cancer forces
you to consider
your entire
existence.
You start to
see life through
new eyes.'

1

HOPE

You'd probably never expect to hear someone say this, but sometimes part of me is actually grateful for having brain cancer. There's beauty in it. It brings things into perspective. It's taught me a lot about life, lessons that I hope to share with you throughout the course of this book. It's taught me to value every moment, it's brought my family and friends closer together, it's introduced me to inspirational people from all over the world and most importantly, it's reminded me that no matter what life throws at us, there's always hope.

I grew up in Bolton and while I had a sense that I was here for a greater purpose, as a kid it didn't feel like there was a lot of opportunity for me to harness that. Despite this, a leap of faith taken during my tumultuous teenage years saw me go from sleeping on couches to joining a major label boy band overnight. As one-fifth of The Wanted I got to travel the world and achieve my dreams. I met my wife Kelsey and we have two beautiful children together. It's a life that I'm proud of, and a life that was perfect, until everything changed in an instant.

In October 2020, at the age of 32, I received the devastating news that I had an inoperable brain tumour. Overnight, my entire world turned upside down and I was forced to re-evaluate the value of life itself.

I soon began to recognise the driving force of my life, a sense of hope that's been present whenever I've found myself in a difficult situation. When there was little belief that I'd ever amount to much, hope motivated me to persevere through the gruelling audition process that even I wasn't sure would get me anywhere. On late nights away from my friends and family, driving through some middle-of-nowhere place in America on a tour bus, hope kept me focused on the fact that fans all over the world wanted to see us perform and who were we to get in the way of that?

Never has that hopefulness been as important following my diagnosis: it gave me the drive to explore treatments that were never offered to me by doctors and helped me to persevere through the brutal side effects of radiotherapy and chemotherapy. I saw it, like a tiny light in the distance, always guiding me to try. As long as I do my best, that's all anyone can ask for. But I have to strive towards that hope. My children, Aurelia and Bodhi, are the personification of this hope. They are always my most important consideration and I hope that they will be able to look back at my journey and see how hope helped me fight against this unimaginable obstacle. By keeping hope at the forefront of my mind, I've already exceeded the expectations that I believe the doctors had for me.

My cancer journey has been a huge learning curve and the more I've educated myself on brain cancer, the broader community and the challenges we face, the more I have a compulsion to make a difference. I believe that by sharing my journey, as honestly as possible, I can help to spread awareness about brain tumours that I think is necessary in order to raise the amount of funding that is given to brain cancer research. I feel like it's my duty to help others through this horrific journey and to do whatever I can to make it a little more palatable.

I believe that the lessons I've learned on this journey extend to everyone, not only those in the broad community of people living with cancer who inspire me every day. No matter what your challenges in life, I hope that the perspective I've gained in the past 18 months can help you to live your life in a more fulfilling way, less hindered by the things that don't matter and with more value placed on the ones that you really care about.

Cancer forces you to consider your entire existence. You start to see life through new eyes. I've completely changed as a person, for the better. It's made me question what my life has been about, what it means, what legacy I'm leaving behind. And I no longer stress about the small things that used to feel so important. Now what matters to me is the times spent with the kids watching TV in the morning, small things like that which are so easily taken for granted. It's important to stay present, absorbing and making the most of every moment.

Before I get any further, I want to acknowledge here that having a tumour in my brain has had a huge impact on my memory. It mainly impacts my short-term memory, so if I'd have told you something ten minutes ago, I might have already forgotten ever saying it by now. As you can probably imagine, this does make the process of writing a book about my life quite tricky and certain details have been very difficult to recall. My aim here has been to try and broadly paint the highs and lows of my life, the lessons I've learned along the way and how my experiences have taught me that we can always be hopeful.

I could not have written this book without the help of other people who have been with me at various stages throughout my life. Those who have helped to bring things into the narrative that I wouldn't have remembered, as hard as I tried! These people include my amazing wife Kelsey, my mum Noreen, my dad Nigel, my brother Lewis, my manager Damien Sanders, my long-suffering tour manager Martin Wright, Dave Bolton – who has been a huge inspiration on my cancer journey, I'll introduce you to him later – and a couple of lads called Max George and Jay McGuiness, who were in a band that you might have heard of: The Wanted. These people have helped make this story all the more vivid and I thank them for taking the time to help me bring it all to life.

When I wake up in the morning I want to be the best version of me that I can be. You never know how quickly life can change, so live today like it's your last. This is not a book about dying, it's about living. It's a book about finding hope in whatever situation you're dealt and living your best life, no matter what.

'I wanted more out of life than putting all of my waking hours into something that I didn't care about.'

2

HOME

Tonge Moor in Bolton is your typical northern working-class suburb. It's a nice safe place to grow up, with plenty of families. If you close your eyes and imagine a suburban cul-de-sac, you're probably imagining something similar to the house I grew up in. From the outside looking in, it's not always the most exciting or inspiring place, but I loved growing up there. The area was given its vibrance and life by the people who inhabit it. People like my mum Noreen, my dad Nigel, my brother Lewis, our next-door neighbours Ronny and Jill and their two daughters. I've struggled to match that sense of community anywhere else that life has taken me.

Mum worked as a weaver in a cotton mill for the textiles

company Dorma and my dad, Nigel, was a cloth cutter. It might sound like something out of *Oliver Twist*, but it was actually quite common in Bolton in the 1960s. In the 18th century, Bolton was an internationally renowned major centre for textile manufacture and is famous for its cotton mills. The humidity in the Northwest, because of all the rain, provided good conditions for the cotton, which is why places like Bolton were developed as industrial towns. Mum describes her career education as being like the scene from the iconic 1969 Ken Loach film *Kes*, where the protagonist Billy Casper attends a youth employment office and is presented with very limited options. Further education just wasn't an option for her: she basically had the choice of a factory or a mill and she chose the latter.

My parents put in long hours of tough manual labour to make sure that my older brother Lewis and I had a roof over our head. They gave us everything we ever asked for, but it wasn't easy for them. Proudly working class, they overcompensated for the struggle they'd had growing up by making sure that there was never anything that we went without. They bought a timeshare in Calahonda, Spain, in the eighties and we went there on holiday every summer. We always had good clothes on our backs and Christmas was pretty excessive: whatever bikes or PlayStations we asked for we'd get, even though I realise now that my mum and dad probably couldn't really afford them. I can only imagine some of the sacrifices that they had to make for us and I really appreciate them for providing us with such a great childhood.

Watching how hard they worked, it was impossible for me not to be aware of the rat race from an early age. That's the best way I can think of to describe how my parents were living, working every hour that God sent in order to make ends meet. Rather than send us to childminders, they arranged their work schedules so that Mum would work weekends and night shifts and Dad would work weekdays. That meant that we always had a parent at home and we spent a lot of time with them individually, though rarely together as a whole family.

By the late 1980s factory production was beginning to decline. Most companies were moving their operations over to China and India to cut down on costs and much of Bolton's cotton trade came to a halt. Luckily my parents both saw it coming: they knew it wouldn't be long before all of the factory jobs were gone. Back in the day people in Bolton would keep a factory job for their entire careers, but my parents had to adapt to the times and pivot into new careers so Dad trained to be a painter and decorator.

I remember doing some work experience with my dad when I was a bit older – I must have been about 15. I'd agreed to help out so that I could earn a bit of money for myself. In the first week he had me sanding down these walls and my hands were in bits. I was like, *I ain't doing this as a job when I get older, fuck that.* I knew I wasn't going to end up doing manual labour, I was determined not to.

'There's no way I'm doing work like that, it's for losers,' I told my mum as I walked into the house one night, throwing my bag down in the hallway.

'Well, it's alright saying that,' she answered wryly, 'but what *are* you going to do?'

The truth is I had no idea.

I think the majority of my youth seemed to revolve more around seeing and experiencing things that I knew I didn't like, which eventually helped me to find the things that I was passionate about. Often I dismissed this and felt like I was wasting time, but there's a lot of value in ruling out the things that don't work for you. It's a helpful part of the process of finding out what does motivate you, which is not always easy to figure out as a teenager.

I also recall visiting Dad at the factory one day and having a similar feeling. A factory really isn't a pleasant environment to be in and thinking about how many hours of the day my dad was spending in that place was heartbreaking. I still wasn't necessarily clear on what I wanted to do for a job, but I knew that I wanted more out of life than putting all of my waking hours into something that I didn't care about. As I've said, I believe that I was put here for a greater purpose, although at that time I had no idea what that might be. If it wasn't for my attitude towards rejecting what was available to me, I probably would never have ended up making much of myself.

While Lewis and I were at school, Mum started to use her days to educate herself further. In the early nineties, she studied for a BTEC, then a degree in English Literature and Gender Studies. It was quite a new area of study at the time and she loved it. She'd always been clever as a child but the mindset she'd been raised with, coming from an impoverished background had become an obstacle for her as a shy kid growing up in Bolton. Completing her degree helped her to challenge that perception she'd had of herself. It helped her to get a better job as a project manager in retail, but what she really wanted to do was teach. Unfortunately, she'd need to be able to take a year out in order to get a teaching qualification and since me and Lewis were her priority she couldn't afford to do that. I really appreciate the sacrifice she made there, even though at the time I don't think I could fully comprehend what that must have been like for her. I'm really proud to say that in 2021, as she turned 60, she did her PGCE and Noreen Parker is now an English teacher.

Probably my favourite part of growing up in Tonge Moor was the sense of community. If you've ever got a problem, your next-door neighbour will know about it and they'll do their best to help you out. Everybody got on with each other. If you ever needed to get hold of me I'd probably have been on a swing in the park at the top of our road. We lived in a cul-de-sac so our street was always quiet and always felt very safe. Kids had a lot more freedom when I was growing up than I think they have now. Mum and Dad would let us roam around free because there were no worries about anything. I used to ride around on my BMX with stunt pegs, trying to do tricks and failing miserably.

Our next-door neighbours Ronny and Jill have emigrated to Australia now, but as a kid I was always in their house, eating their food and chatting away to them. They had two daughters who were around the same age as me and Lewis and our parents were good friends. They felt like an extension of our family and I loved being able to go back and forth between the two houses. Ronny and Jill actually lived together for years before they got married and when they did eventually decide to tie the knot, they invited me to sing at their wedding. It was such an honour for me to do that for them and my way to pay back just a tiny bit for all of their hospitality and friendship.

As far as I can remember, I was a very happy child. Always active, very energetic even from being tiny. I could walk from ten months old, demanded a lot of attention and wanted to play with anyone who came into my vicinity. Wherever I went, I was going at 100 miles an hour and when I was two years old, I collided with the patio doors, gashing open my head and leaving a scar that I have today. Contrary to the famous saying, I definitely

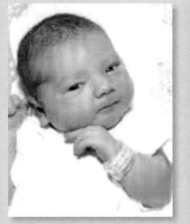

Baby Tom!

Always the cheekiest in the room.

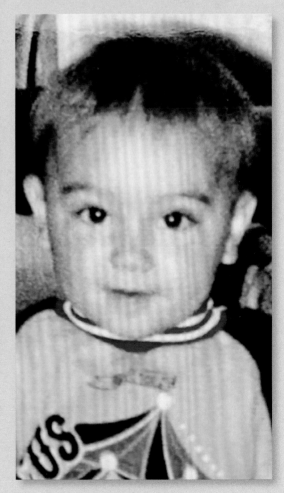

Me and my brother, Lewis.

A perfectly innocent choirboy at school, and at 16, below, looking completely different... Who knew what was just round the corner for me?

Left: The boys! Siva, me, Jay, Nathan and Max, backstage at the Help For Heroes Concert at Twickenham.

Right: Me and Jay loving performing in Tokyo, Japan, in 2013.

Right: Detroit, USA, in 2014, having an amazing time performing on our Word of Mouth world tour.

Below: Onstage at Capital FM's Summertime Ball at Wembley Stadium.

The amazing fans at Fusion Festival in Birmingham, 2014, and below at the E! 2013 Upfront in Manhattan, New York. I had so many incredible trips and opportunities with the boys and The Wanted. When you get the opportunity to thank those who helped put you on the stage, you've got to do it!

Chicago, USA, in 2013, having the time of my life, and then in Brighton a few months later.

Trying to chat Kelsey up when we first met all those years ago... To all the adventures we shared together. Thank you, Kelsey, for being mine.

Left and below: Our wedding day, and what we made.

Me and my brilliant mum, Noreen.

think I learned to run before I could walk. On one holiday to Malta, when I was five, my mum recalls that she couldn't relax because I used to charge around the pool area like a madman.

I've always been very inquisitive about the world around me and Mum says that I'd ask a thousand questions a day. I think that curiosity is still with me today – I like to know how things work and what's going on around me. Back then I always wanted to know what the adults were talking about and would stick my nose into their business whenever I could.

I'll admit now that sometimes my gossiping could cause a bit of trouble. When I was about seven, Ronny and Jill had got themselves some lights in the back garden. It was all the rage at the time, so they went and got some and Ronny put them up himself. They were always making improvements to their house and I think that my dad might have been a little bit jealous because he wasn't much of a handyman himself. One afternoon I wandered into the back room and saw Dad having a nosey out of the window into their garden.

'I don't think I like them lights that Jill and Ronny have put up there. They look a bit cheap and tacky to me,' he said.

It can't have been an hour later that I was over in the garden next door and Ronny was proudly showing off his newest purchase.

'What do you think of our lights?' he asked, beaming.

'Ah, me dad says they look cheap and tacky,' I replied.

Needless to say, my parents could have killed me after sharing that and they had to go round grovelling. They've since said that they soon realised that they needed to be very careful about what they said around me because they never knew what would catch my attention and what I might share elsewhere.

I think I was first introduced to music by my mum. She was a huge fan and music was her life. You couldn't come into our household without being indoctrinated into becoming a Genesis fan. Mum was into a broad range of stuff – she liked a lot of classics but also prided herself on being up to date with the latest releases. We'd have definitely denied it at the time, but she was the one who introduced us to the Manic Street Preachers – who have been a huge influence on both me and my brother – when she bought their album. As a child, I used to sing all of the time too; I loved it. I knew loads of Motown classics and Beatles songs that my mum would play around the house or in the car.

My other passion, like most boys growing up in areas like Tonge Moor, was football – I was obsessed with it. It was my escape from reality and one of the few ways I could think of at the time that would allow me to escape the rat race mentality.

Football was huge in our household. We had a season

ticket for Bolton Wanderers so we used to go to Burnden
Park on a Saturday for the match. I have fond memories
of being there. They used to have pies and me and my
brother would be wearing the full kit. We loved it. It was
such a great overall feeling. There was a player called
Eiður Guðjohnsen who then ended up signing for Chelsea
and becoming a bit of a superstar. As a kid I really looked
up to him, he was a personal hero of mine.

I remember celebrating every birthday with a football
party in the main hall at Canon Slade, a local school up
the road from where I lived. I had a shelf full of mini-
cups that I'd won from those, normally claiming victory
by scoring a penalty against some other kid's dad in a
shootout. As I started to get older, I was convinced that it
was my calling to play professionally.

Every Sunday I'd lace up my boots for a local team
called Oxford Grove. I played for them for about ten
years, between the ages of 7 and 17. There was a guy that
ran the team called Shawn Danby, he was a great guy and
a great football coach. His son Martin played on the team
as well. Everyone at Oxford Grove was a year younger
than me, but I was so small that I could never compete
at my own age level. I always had to play a year below
because I was a little peanut. It didn't bother me at the
time because I just loved getting to play so much.

I was into sports in general and aside from football I
dabbled in rugby and gymnastics but I soon realised my

limitations in rugby because of my size. I used to have to drag bigger lads in front of me to protect myself, but I was fast so I made a good fly-half for a while.

But I was really good at gymnastics. My mum had seen an advert for an after-school gymnastics club at the local school and thought it might be a good way for me to get rid of some excess energy. I'm good at observing things and then being able to mimic them myself, which really showed through when I was learning gymnastics. Later in life when I was participating in *The Jump*, a winter sports competition on Channel 4, the coaches noticed this too. They said that if I'd trained from a young age I could have had a career as a professional skier, because I picked it up so naturally. I think that if I'd have stuck to gymnastics I would probably have been quite successful in that too, but unfortunately when I got to secondary school I ended up quitting because I thought I was too cool for it! Now looking back, it's one of those things that I wish I had stuck with because I enjoyed it, rather than being so bothered about trying to fit in with what other people thought about me.

I went back to concentrating on football and like so many other boys at that age I dreamed of making it my career. As I got a bit older I started to realise that the opportunity wasn't coming and so I began to fall out of love with it. It was time to move on; I was just playing for fun by the end but that doesn't mean it wasn't without its lessons. When I first started playing as a young kid I was always so selfish on the ball, I never used to pass. I wanted the time to shine and I would prioritise having the ball in my possession over anything else. During my decade at Oxford Grove I learned that this wasn't a good quality though: it soon became clear to me that hogging the ball wasn't getting us the wins we needed to do well in the league. I had to accept that playing football wasn't about me, teamwork gets results. The real marker of success was consistency for the team as a whole, rather than showing off and getting attention. So, I became a team player and I think that really stuck with me. It's gone on to serve me well and I think being able to work well with others is something that we should all strive for.

'I learned the
hard way that
the key to a
more fulfilling
lifestyle is to
be yourself.'

3

SCHOOL

St Brendan's RC Primary School was in Harwood, which is a really nice area with big houses and a lot of my friends were from there. My mum had gone to the same school and she loved her time there so she sent me and Lewis. Every morning, she would drop me off at my aunt's house early and then I'd walk to school with my cousin. I used to walk around St Brendan's feeling like I was in this really posh place compared to what I was used to at home.

Although I'm not religious anymore, as a kid I did believe in God. I was raised Catholic. Less because it was something that my parents subscribed to strongly, but more because socially, it was what a lot of the people in our community did and I was attending a Catholic school.

We used to go to church every Sunday and as a child, I sang in the choir and was even an altar boy. I used to bring the Holy Communion out for the priest and I really enjoyed the sense of responsibility that came with it. I think that role helped me to calm down: an altar boy couldn't be rampaging around the way that I'd been used to. You had to be disciplined and I think that helped me to focus a little bit.

Religion also instilled me with good values. I think on a subconscious level a lot of that is still with me, although now I'd probably consider it more spirituality than religion. It's helpful to have other influences and positive role models in your life as a young kid and I think that I got some of that from spending time at the church.

There were only 18 kids in my year at St Brendan's so we became quite a close group and the teachers had a lot of time for us. I had a teacher in reception called Mrs Allan, who I loved. She was small with long hair and little glasses and I remember her being very kind. Coming from a very loving family, I was surrounded by kindness and have always responded very well to that.

Our headteacher Mrs Thornton was also really lovely, although she was also quite strict. Looking back, I think that was probably very healthy for me. I was always causing some sort of mess or starting fights and I think that she planted the seeds that would help me to start pulling myself together later in life when it really started to matter.

I remember one teacher's punishment was to make us go and stand in a little round bin in the class. That was a bit bizarre now that I think back to it! Needless to say, I spent a fair share of my time making up for all of the nonsense I'd caused and the image of an annoyed young Tom in a bin does make me laugh now.

Although I struggled to achieve academically and school was never my thing, I really loved my primary school experience because it felt so different to being in Tonge Moor. However, at times being perceived differently to some of the other kids would catch up with me.

I remember the St Brendan's leaving do, our record of achievement night: a celebration of how much we'd grown and all of the great memories we'd created during our time at the school. The priest called me up alongside another lad called James.

'What are you going to do when you grow up, James?'

James was middle class and his family were very well regarded at the school. Very disciplined and smart, he did everything he was told, whereas I would let my curiosity get the better of me. If there was something I was interested in happening in another classroom, there's a fair chance that I might wander off over there to investigate. I thought it was fine, I didn't actually realise I was doing anything wrong.

'I bet you're going to become the prime minister!' The priest answered his own question before even giving

James a chance to speak. Then he turned his attention towards me.

'Tom Parker, everyone,' he announced. 'Tom is a nice young lad. He's either going to be a footballer, or he's going to end up in Strangeways.'

All the parents gasped.

Afterwards, my mum grabbed me up out of that school hall and before I knew it, I was stood next to her in the headteacher's office opposite Mrs Thornton and the priest. She fucking absolutely let rip! After facing her wrath the two of them apologised. At the time I didn't even know what the priest had meant by the whole thing. Luckily, as an 11-year-old, the reference went over my head – I had no idea that Strangeways was the original name of HM Prison Manchester.

It was only a joke, but my mum was absolutely livid and rightly so. The priest was mortified and very apologetic when she explained why she was so offended. Knowing my mum's background, it is understandable that she took issue with this kind of deprecating humour. She'd grown up fighting against low expectations and the mentality that comes with growing up poor, her whole life. She had to learn to believe in herself. No one put any effort or energy into her because she was just one of the poor kids from the council estate at that school.

Mum thought that by getting on the property ladder and buying her own house, me and Lewis wouldn't be made to feel the way that she had. The last thing she wanted was for someone to impose those kinds of negative feelings on us after all of the hard work she and Dad had put in to give us a better life than they'd had. Unfortunately, I was well aware of those low expectations that were placed on me by others outside of the home, they were unavoidable. I just didn't fit into society's idea of what a good kid was – I was curious, hands-on, excitable and full of energy, while the staff at school wanted kids to be quiet, obey orders and achieve well academically. Luckily the judgemental way in which I was often perceived was nowhere near as damaging as it might have been, thanks to the confidence and self-belief that Mum worked so hard to instill in us.

Formal education was never for me, I didn't have the personality type for it – I was more into practical things and there wasn't much of that at school. I was obviously capable and could teach myself things when I really applied myself, but the style of teaching just didn't work for me. I wanted to be out in the streets playing football. A bit of a wild kid, I wasn't up for sitting down and staying in one position – I always wanted to be active, to be outside.

Secondary school was a particularly tough time in my life. While my attendance at Thornleigh Salesian College was near-perfect, I still wasn't well behaved and would often get the blame for distracting my classmates. I didn't feel that support and kindness from the teachers that I'd had at St Brendans and to make matters worse, all the other kids were growing fast while I remained the short kid, making me an easy target for bullying.

My first year wasn't so bad, but I started wanting to fit in with the cool crowd. I began to hide parts of myself, things that didn't contribute towards the image that I wanted to portray to others: I stopped doing gymnastics, I stopped singing as much, I didn't talk to my parents as much about what I was going through. There are always consequences of trying to fit in with something that isn't authentically you and I learned the hard way that the key to a more fulfilling lifestyle is to be yourself. I had to put up with a lot of shit in order to be accepted by the popular kids – shit that, looking back, wasn't worth putting up with. It wasn't overtly bullying, but a general toxicity, a set of unspoken conditions that had to be adhered to in order to hold a place in the group. Once I got into that mindset, it was very difficult to get back out of it.

There was a lot of name calling because of my height. I used to wear a parka, which led to me being nicknamed Saj after the kid from the film *East Is East*. I literally wasn't called Tom throughout the whole of school. It might not seem like a huge deal, but looking back, I can see it was such a constant reminder of my peers' disrespect, it was emotionally draining. It was tough, but I just had to get on with it. That was what people called me and that was that. Sometimes you just have to be a little bit resilient in order to get through stuff.

The final straw came when my backpack full of GCSE work was stolen in Year 11 and it took me a week to get it back. By the time I discovered my notes all over the muddy cricket pitch, none of it was readable anymore. I couldn't hold back the tears when my mum found out about it. At that point in my life I rarely cried, which made it especially apparent how much all of this stuff had been building up and affecting me. But that finally made me snap out of chasing the cool crowd. I was in over my head; I realised that I'd been conforming to what other people wanted, rather than being myself. For the rest of the year I reconnected with a group of kids that I'd been with in primary school, who accepted me for who I was, and it was by far the best part of my secondary school experience.

It's important not to change ourselves in order to be accepted by others, but to be true to who we really are. It's not worth jumping through hurdles to impress other people when we could be enjoying a much more fulfilled life by listening to our own needs and beliefs. That second group of kids are the ones that I'd known through the whole of school and they had always been there for me, even after I'd gone off trying to be one of the 'popular' kids. Had I stayed true to myself and stuck by them, my whole secondary school experience might have been much more positive.

If I had known the low expectations that people had for me, it could have really affected my confidence and I'm glad that it didn't. Looking back, I realise that it's really important that we don't take to heart the judgements that others make of us. Just because they can't see our potential, that shouldn't stop us from aspiring to what we believe is achievable.

'Through my
self-discovery
and
experimentation,
I started to
find my voice.'

4

MUSIC

From a young age I had drive and ambition in me. I wanted to do something different, I wasn't going to accept the options that were presented to me – I knew there was more. I just needed to find out what it was that I was passionate about.

My brother Lewis is five years older than me and was actually the first musician in our family. He's a guitarist and has played in a few different bands over the years. Growing up, he'd play in clubs and bars around the local area and I used to love going to watch him. Lewis had a very direct influence on me and I was obsessed with indie rock music initially because he was.

I remember like it was yesterday: 14 years old, sneaking

into Lewis' room while he was out and picking up his guitar. Even holding it in my hands filled me with excitement – the endless possibilities that were at my fingertips in those six strings.

Although Lewis was the one who taught me my first chords to get me going, I think he'd have killed me if he'd caught me messing about with his prized possession like that. The mischievous streak in me probably got a bit of a kick out of that too. When we were young, our relationship was a tough one – five years is quite a big gap and at times it was difficult for us both to manage. I think that because I was younger I'd steal the limelight off him a little and that caused a bit of tension between us. It wasn't until I got older that we started to get along.

When I got interested in something, I would give it everything. A little bit more than most, who might balance it with other things. I would be quite extreme and that would be all that I would think about. When I started to envisage myself as a future rock star, like my heroes, then I knew I had to put everything into the guitar.

We didn't have access to the internet at that point in my life, so I had to go through books to teach myself to play guitar. I practised whenever I had the chance to steal a moment until eventually I had taught myself to play 'Wonderwall' by Oasis. That song kick-started my whole interest in music. If it wasn't for Oasis, I genuinely don't know whether I'd have made it to the music industry –

they were that influential to my life. As working-class lads from Manchester with huge aspirations, I could really relate to them. You grow up with no expectations of what your life is going to be, but when you see success stories like Oasis, you kind of go, 'Well, if they can do it, I can do it too.' I remember learning their songs on guitar and being inspired to persevere. I started to realise that maybe music was the outlet that I'd been looking for since I was in primary school. This is what I was meant to do, it felt like a calling.

The Manic Street Preachers were the first band I ever listened to and I also loved Stereophonics. All those gravelly voices, I really gravitated towards them. Through self-discovery and experimentation, I started to find my voice. I'd already been in the choir when I was at St Brendans so I knew I could sing, but this felt different – this was my own self-expression, it was like a release for me.

After I'd learned to play a few of the songs by bands that I liked, I started to experiment with writing songs of my own. The first one I ever wrote was called 'Let It Go' and it was very personal to me. I recorded it at home and put it on my MySpace – you might still be able to find it on there. I loved songwriting, but I think that singing and performing the songs always came ahead of that for me, particularly at that time. I went back to it now and then though, contributing to writing on songs for The Wanted and producing dance music for Lost + Found. All of that stuff stems from just being a restless kid sat at home with a guitar and a great passion for music.

When I started to tell my friends about my interest in singing, I had completely the opposite reaction than you might expect from a group of northern lads. At that point my two best friends were Ali and Yara. They have been incredibly important to me throughout my life and I'm still in contact with them now. Ali used to have a black Citroën Saxo and he'd drive me and Yara so the three of us could smoke weed in the car. We used to take a guitar and sit there and sing. Ali would always be like, 'Fucking hell, mate, you've got a good voice. You should use this more.' He was the first person to believe in me. I never really thought much of it at the time, but his motivation has come through at some very crucial points in my life and he has had a profound effect on me.

Despite my negative secondary school experience, when it came to leaving day at Thornleigh, I decided to put myself forward to sing. When the time came, I was shitting my pants, but I had this feeling that singing was something I was supposed to be doing – like it was my destiny. And I had the support of Ali and Yara behind me so that spurred me on a bit as well. It was the first time I'd sung in public since I was in the choir at St Brendans and I was so nervous standing there, looking at all of the students in the entire school. I think that might still be the most nervous I've ever felt about singing and I went on to play in front of 20,000 people at The O2 Arena! That school performance ended up being a massive turning point for me, though. People were coming up to me afterwards, impressed, surprised and excited at how good my performance was. I realised that despite all of the academic work I'd struggled with in that building, what I was walking away with was the dream of becoming a singer. I didn't know exactly how I was going to make it happen yet, but at least I'd figured out what my goal was.

Unfortunately, a teenager in Bolton wasn't exactly inundated with options for pursuing a career in music so I decided to try the only avenue I was aware of as a 16-year-old and audition for *The X Factor*. I got the train over to Manchester for the audition and joined the massive queue of other hopefuls waiting on a drizzly morning for their chance to shine in front of the judges. Sadly, I wouldn't even make it that far.

I showed up and sang my heart out in front of the producers. I'd been practising a cover of Westlife's 'Flying Without Wings', which in hindsight probably wasn't the best song choice – they must have heard it hundreds of times per series. But I showed up and gave it my best shot. Because so many people audition for *The X Factor*, there are actually a few rounds that aren't televised before you even get to face Simon Cowell and co, and I didn't make it past those. At the time I was devastated. My only saving grace was that they hadn't recorded my rejection.

I remember being so glad that at least they didn't have it on film because it was a really difficult rejection for me to shake off. I couldn't help wondering whether the show's producers were right. Maybe I was being delusional about my dreams. It was a huge knock to my confidence and I stopped singing for about six months after that – I'd tried the only route I knew into the music industry and they didn't want me.

Now looking back, there are so many reasons why the producers might have rejected me, many of which were completely out of my control, and I'm glad that I managed to shake that criticism and not let that be the end of my journey. I think that it's important to learn how to take feedback, whether it's negative or positive, and not to allow it to affect your life and whatever you're working on too much. Everyone has their own journey towards a goal and everybody is different so it's important to stay on the path you've set for yourself and not be swayed too much by what other people think about it.

In the privacy of my own home, I remained dedicated to singing and practising guitar, so after a while, once the self-doubt from my experience at *The X Factor* was beginning to fade, I began to think about performing again. This time I decided maybe I'd try somewhere a bit smaller, somewhere local.

A mate of my dad's knew the people who ran The VBQ, a pub on Blackburn Road in Bolton, and they were happy to have me come down and play a few songs. The room was packed out that night. All my friends and family were mingling around the regulars, who were probably pretty confused by what was going on at first. I played some covers, including Linkin Park's 'Numb' and a few of my usual go-tos like 'Wonderwall'. By the end of my set I had everyone singing along with me. It was such an adrenaline rush, the best I'd had at that point. That pub gig reaffirmed that music was what I wanted to do and helped me build some confidence back.

Ever since that day, no matter where my travels have taken me, the stage has felt like home to me; whether it's been a local pub or an international stadium, it's remained my place to thrive. The moment I step out in front of an audience, ready to share my gift, I feel at home.

I was sitting on the sofa watching TV one evening when my mum came in from work.

'What are you going to do, Tom?' she asked, dumping her bag down next to me. 'You're either going to college then on to university, or you're going to have to get a job. These are your options at 16.'

'I don't want to go to university,' I snapped back.

'Well, are you going to get a job?'

'I might do.'

In reality, I didn't want to do anything other than sit around smoking weed!

'Well, if you get a job, you can start paying some keep money,' Mum replied. She wanted me to go down the education route because she hadn't had that opportunity herself when she was my age, and she knew this would deter me from getting a job.

'What's keep money?' I asked.

'You give me some money towards the food and all the bills.'

'You what? You want me to give you money, my own mum and dad?' I couldn't get my head around it, I was shocked. 'No, that can't be right!'

'Yeah, it is. If you start working and making money, you need to contribute.'

I decided there was no way I was giving money to my own parents so I enrolled in Smithills College. Mum and Dad were funding me to keep me going, so it was the easier of the two options for a while until I ended up getting kicked out because I wasn't turning up. The money my parents had been giving me was intended for buses and dinner, but I was just spending it on weed instead and hanging around Tonge Moor with my mates.

I did eventually end up getting a couple of part-time jobs. One at McDonald's, where I didn't last two minutes, and for a while my mum was working at New Look so she got me a job in the men's department. I used to get ready for work, put my uniform on, get my parents to give me a lift into town and then not bother going in.

I don't know how it happened, but somehow despite all of that I got an unconditional offer to study geography at Manchester Met. To this day I think it must have been a mistake. I got two Ds and an E at A-level! When the results came in, I was on holiday in Bulgaria with my girlfriend at the time and my dad called me and said, 'Thomas, you've failed!' Miraculously, it didn't matter because the unconditional offer meant that I had a place regardless of my grades.

I was pretty good at geography and it was the one subject that I quite enjoyed at school, but, unsurprisingly, I only ended up lasting six months before I fucked it off. I'd been living at home in Bolton, rather than broadening my horizons and getting the full university experience. I was constantly waking up and not having the drive to attend, so I'd call the boys and go for a beer instead. I'd used my student status to get as much money as I could, maxing out my student overdraft and squandering my student loan in a couple of weeks. By the February I had to call Manchester Met and defer my studies until September because I'd fallen too far behind on work. But by the time September came, I'd totally moved on from any ideas about being a university student so I ended up with a load of debt to pay back, but nothing to show for it.

Again, I just didn't feel education was for me. The

education system in this country, particularly when I was growing up, was limited to suit certain subjects and learning styles. It didn't offer me a way to engage with the things I was really passionate about, I wasn't inspired and therefore it always felt more like an obstacle or a chore to me. That system doesn't work for everyone although I did try continuously to push through. At Thornleigh I never even thought I was going to go to college, never mind university, but after that six months I was at the end of the road in terms of formal education.

I think another key moment that steered me towards the possibility of making a career in music was actually a karaoke competition that I entered at a pub in Bolton called The Swan. The pub put up a £1,000 cash prize and so it was packed out. I was still only 16 and I had decided that I was going to enter, so a bunch of us went down, including my parents, Ali and Yara. My mum was sick outside the pub because she was so nervous for me! The atmosphere was electric after my performance of the Elton John and George Michael duet, 'Don't Let The Sun Go Down On Me' – to this day, Mum can't listen to that song without bursting into tears. I remember all the regulars seeming quite pissed off that some boy from Tonge Moor had turned up and stole their thunder. Anyway, I walked away with the £1,000 – and used it to start growing weed!

There was a guy in the audience there who was part of Take That II, a tribute act based in Leeds. They were looking for a Mark Owen to complete their line-up and saw some potential in me, so they put me in touch with a guy called Tim Barron, who was managing the group. Joining that band gave me my first taste of having to go and sing in public as part of a group. It also opened my eyes to the fact that making a career out of singing wasn't so far-fetched as it had seemed when I'd been rejected from *The X Factor*. Most importantly, I think it instilled a bit of discipline into me.

It was a pretty serious operation, being part of a tribute act, and we'd get bookings all over – mainly to perform for middle-aged men in working men's clubs. I remember in particular the guy who played Gary Barlow basically lived as Gary Barlow – it was pretty bizarre, to be honest. But I was being paid for singing and I would much rather have been doing that than manual labour. As a typical teenager, I would stroll to meetings and rehearsals at my leisure, thinking I could talk my way out of any consequences due to my bad punctuality. There was one night when we had a gig in Wrexham and we needed to meet up in Leeds to catch a bus that had been hired to take us to the show.

'If you don't turn up on time, I'm going without you,' Tim warned me.

They couldn't possibly turn up to play as Take That without Mark, I thought to myself. So I agreed that if I wasn't on time, I understood there would no longer be a bus there to transport me the two-hour drive to Wrexham and I didn't think much more of it.

Imagine my surprise when I arrived at the meeting point to discover that the threat hadn't been as hollow as I'd assumed. The bus had left and I had to figure out my way, alone, paying out of my own pocket for a last-minute train. I remember making it just in the nick of time to join the rest of the group on stage and making a mental note to myself never to be late again.

Tim Barron was a no-nonsense Yorkshireman who had quite a lasting effect on me. He taught me how to handle myself in the business and to take my career more seriously. I learned from him that if I wanted to be successful in music, I had to treat it like any other job so I started to approach my singing career in a much more professional manner.

The experience of being in Take That II was a huge turning point that helped me to get past the doubts I'd been having and my difficulties with the education system. I started to take opportunities more seriously and understand that all of these experiences were important in working towards my future. It taught me that with a bit of focus, effort and discipline I could make something of myself. I didn't have to go along with the low expectations that seemed to follow me through society, instead I could make my dreams of a music career come true.

'I made sure I had a positive attitude and I did my best. I wanted to show that I was willing to put in the hard work, whatever it took.'

5

AUDITIONS

After I was kicked out of uni, things continued to become more and more chaotic at home. I spent as much time outdoors in the park as I could and, to the disappointment of my parents, my weed habit started to become a problem. Looking back, their reaction was totally understandable. The honest truth is that my habit became very destructive in my teenage years – I became someone totally different and actually somebody who wasn't very nice. My parents are quite liberal-minded, but they couldn't accept the person that I was becoming and we had a lot of arguments about my cannabis usage. Over the space of a couple of years I'd gone from casually smoking with my mates to full-on addiction. We would do pretty much anything to get high. I'm ashamed to say that eventually extended to taking stuff from my parents' house and pawning it at Cash Converters: videos, jewellery, anything that could get me a few quid. That's how much I'd lost control of who I was.

The final straw came when somebody posted a birthday card through the door for Mum. I opened it and stole the crisp ten-pound notes that had been folded inside. My parents had to take extreme measures in the hope that I might learn to understand the damaging path that I was on: they kicked me out of our family home.

My mum couldn't bring herself to do it and had to get my dad to break the news to me. I can't say I blame them – I was the sort of person who wasn't responsive to threats. For them to make a difference to me, they were going to have to follow through. No amount of talking would work so Dad sat me down and broke the news that I would no longer be allowed to live in the house. I was like, 'Fuck, where am I living?'

I ended up on a sofa in my mate Wayne's house around the corner for the next few months. Living with Wayne was very messy – him and his housemates liked to party and given the fact that their couch was also my bed, those parties were inescapable for me. Not that I was trying to escape them. It was probably the worst place for me at that time, but as a teenager I couldn't see that. I continued this downward spiral: more weed, more drink, and I wouldn't see my parents even though they were only a couple of streets away.

During the summer of 2008, Ali, who had been living in Sheffield for university, came to one of the parties. He saw where I was living and suggested it might be fun if I came and crashed at his student flat. I loved living with Ali – I got to live the life of a student every day without having to study. We were having a great time, even though I had absolutely nothing going for me in the way of a job, or even any real aspirations.

I think it was fate that drew me to discover an advert for a site called Jayne Collins Casting. They were looking for people to audition for a pop group. I was on Jobseeker's Allowance, trying to figure out what my next step would be, so I applied to audition and the very next day, me and Ali were on the motorway in his Citroën Saxo – fuelled by stolen petrol – racing down to London for what I felt could be the opportunity I'd been craving. On the long drive down, I felt as though I was moving towards my destiny. Both of us did, Ali and I were laser focused on the mission – we believed that this was meant to happen.

People like Ali didn't need to believe in me and they weren't getting anything out of it personally, but they did and for that, I'll forever be grateful. Driving me to London was something he did off his own back, just because he thought I could be successful as a singer. It's really lovely that I've had those kinds of relationships in my life and it just goes to show that often you don't realise what a huge impact you're making on the lives of those around you just by being yourself. Without Ali being the good person he is, I might never have achieved half the things I have in life.

I arrived at a church hall in north London to meet a man called David, who was running the first round of auditions. I was wearing a tracksuit with my hood up, so I didn't exactly look the part for what you'd expect from a boy band, particularly at that time. After the success at the karaoke competition I sang 'Don't Let The Sun Go Down On Me' again as well as a personal favourite, 'Handbags And Gladrags' by Stereophonics – which I played on guitar – because that one really suits my voice. I learned from *The X Factor* audition that it's important to always be true to yourself; these were songs that really resonated with me and you can hear that in a performance. They were the songs that would give me the best chance and after the effort that Ali and I had put in to make it to the audition, I had to give it my all. I took a bit of a risk by throwing in 'Let It Go', the first original song that I'd written myself – I think that it showed how confident I was in my ability and gave a sense of my passion for music.

David didn't give anything away after my performance. I just got back in the car with Ali, totally unaware of how well I'd done. It was my first experience of the auditioning process and so I really had no expectations, but I felt good that I'd given a strong performance that reflected who I am.

Shortly after that I was notified they wanted to see me again and the next few months were consumed with driving up and down the country for round after round of auditions. Things started to get particularly difficult for me when they began to incorporate dance. You'd turn up and learn some brand new choreography that you'd never seen before and then after a few practice runs have to perform it back. Dancing is not my thing! I was embarrassed about that, but I'd come so far through the process already and I wasn't about to give up. After a crash course from my cousin Vicky, a trained dancer who gave me lessons for free in Bolton, I showed up at the audition, found myself a space in the hall near the front and tried to be as open-minded as possible. I think that willingness is what helped me to progress through those stages of the audition. I wasn't the best dancer there by any means, but I made sure I had a positive attitude and I did my best. I wanted to show that I was willing to put in the hard work, whatever it took. That can be applied to so many things in life: if you keep going, you'll make it. Believe in yourself hard enough, approach any challenge with a good mental attitude, stay open-minded to giving things a try and just do your best. That's all we can really ask of ourselves.

Over the space of nine months over 1,000 people

took their chance at a place in the yet-to-be-named pop group. It was being assembled by Jayne Collins, who had previously formed the massively successful group The Saturdays. Jayne was very eccentric and so was Rob, her husband, who was going to be managing the band. They were very posh, unlike anyone that I'd really come into contact with at that point, but they were really lovely. Even during the audition process I could tell that they really cared and they'd always do whatever they could to provide for us. You have to have patience to want to work with five young lads and launch a career with them. Reflecting on it now, I took that patience for granted and didn't appreciate it at the time. Particularly during those early stages when I was a little bit lost in life, the support and patience of people around me – from family and friends to Jayne and Rob – were imperative in helping me to stand up and make something of myself.

During that time I started to heal my relationship with my parents and I moved back to Tonge Moor. Living on a sofa and partying every night can only get you so far and I realised that I needed to sort my life out.

At a crucial point in the process Ali was busy with university and he'd already gone above and beyond racking up miles in that Saxo, driving me to auditions on an almost-weekly basis. I called my mum and asked if I could have my birthday money early so that I could get the train to London for the next audition but she thought that

I was going down to get pissed with Ali and Yara, or the entire audition process was an elaborate scam altogether! She said that if I was dedicated to it, then I'd take the bus. So I made the £1 Megabus trip.

Sometimes you just feel like things are meant to be and that was one of those times: even though I was cramped in a Megabus seat for seven hours, I knew it was the right thing to do. I genuinely don't know what it was that pushed me to keep going, but there was something within me that was driving me forward. I was going with my gut, which I think is as good a reason as any to do something. Our gut feelings are a very powerful tool – they take account of all of the experiences we've had and urge us to make decisions based on what feels best for us.

On the way down to the final audition I had to change at Manchester and saw a guy on the platform that looked familiar – he had that 'bad boy' look that was perfect for a boy band. I had a feeling he'd been in one of my auditions so I wandered over to him. He'd obviously seen me and thought the same.

'How are you doing?' He smiled, reaching out to shake my hand. 'I'm Max. Are you going to the audition?'

We sat together for the journey down and neither of us really knew that much about what we were getting into. Max had been in a few bands before, so he was familiar with the process whereas it was all very new to me. I used the opportunity to ask him lots of questions about the music industry. We had a similar sense of humour, coming from the North West, and it felt comforting to know that someone else from a similar area was being considered for the group too.

By that stage they had narrowed us down to 12 and after that audition they picked the final five, which I was part of. I couldn't believe it: all of that work and self-belief was paying off. Following my gut had led me to where I needed to be but my celebration didn't last long.

For some reason there were some second thoughts and we were brought back in for another audition. They were potentially going to change the final five for another line-up. I think it was me that they weren't sure about. I'm guessing that they were wondering whether a working-class lad from Bolton was the right person to complete their vision for Britain's next big boy band. The rest of the boys were more experienced than me and they all seemed pretty comfortable during the audition process. I remember them saying that I was in the final five and not really being able to comprehend what that even meant at that stage – particularly since we'd already had one false start. But within a month we were looking at properties in London as a band. I was definitely part of this new boy band that was about to begin its journey towards pop superstardom.

Everyone at home was a bit taken aback. The expect-ations of me auditioning for the band were very low and so suddenly when I'd made it through and I told my parents that they were moving us into a house in London, they were shocked.

'What? And they're paying for it?'

'Yeah!'

Mum didn't believe any of it until months later when she had a copy of our first single, 'All Time Low', in her hands!

It turns out that actually we were paying for the rent and expenses through our record deal, but we didn't know that at the time. Back then it was all very surreal – I didn't really understand what was being offered to me, but I was happy to take it. Suddenly not having to think about where my next meal was coming from or whose sofa I'd be crashing on opened up a whole new world of opportunity to me.

Now that I look back on it, that whole process was quite a brave thing to do that I didn't give myself credit for: moving to a new city with new people that you've never really met. It was a pretty big deal actually, but being young and having nothing else going on, I just went along with it. That was my opportunity and my moment, and I had to make it happen.

In the end the gruelling process of auditioning was well worth the effort that I'd put in. I was a teenager with no prospects who was suddenly moving to London to join a band signed to Geffen Records.

Sometimes it does take that leap of faith to reach our potential in life. My friends could have called me crazy when I told them I wanted to drive down to London to audition for a boy band. They could so easily have mocked me for it and talked me out of it, but it had interested me and I decided to take the risk of potentially being laughed at or embarrassed by my mates and to give it a go. I'm thankful that they supported me, but even if they hadn't, the fire inside me was urging me to try it and I like to think I'd have done it anyway. If not, I'm certain I'd have regretted it. Had I not made it into the band at the end of it all, those experiences were still incredibly valuable ones and would have helped me figure out my next steps.

The audition process helped me to develop that all-important resilience.

'Getting to
know my four
bandmates,
who would later
become brothers
to me, was
easily one of the
highlights of
my life.'

6

THE WANTED

As rapidly as my life had fallen down, it was picking back up. I had gone from sofa surfing in Sheffield to living in an apartment in London, with the most money I'd ever had in my life and four new roommates. I didn't even know what a record deal meant at that point, but I was like, 'Free money? Yes, please! And a house to live in?' I was buzzing! I felt like the luckiest man in the world.

Although it might seem unusual, finding a new flat to move into with four people I didn't know turned out to be more straightforward than expected. We only looked at a couple of places before we settled on a house in Wandsworth, southwest London. Looking back, I think we just couldn't believe our luck and would probably have said yes to pretty much anything. I lived up in the attic and me and Max put a ping-pong table in the front room that we used to hammer every day – we got so good at it.

Despite having spent 19 years living in the North, at that point moving to London felt so natural to me and I loved being in this house with these lads who were all preparing to set out on this journey together. We were there to build chemistry for the band and it came very easily: there was a natural bond between us all.

Getting to know my four bandmates, who would later become brothers to me, was easily one of the highlights of my life. We had our youngest, cute member of the band, Nathan Sykes, who was still in school when we were getting started. Max George was almost like our dad, he had the most experience in the music industry at the time. Jay McGuiness was our little goofball – he always knew how to make us laugh and kept us in good spirits – and Siva Kaneswaran was the most handsome man that I've ever met – he had actually been working towards a career in modelling, but I'm glad he ended up in the band with us lot instead!

I think that living together really highlighted the individuality that each of us brought to the band; we were all so different. Max and I were extremely outgoing and had been partying since we were about 14, so we kept that energy going. I was definitely the loudest! Then on the other end of the spectrum, you'd have Siva and Nathan, who were happy spending time alone in their rooms. Siva would have silk sheets and candles – he loved watching *Star Trek* and reading. Nathan was still too young for going out, so we'd feel a bit of a responsibility to look after him. We'd all sit around together watching *The Office* or whatever reality TV shows were on at the time and we'd have loads of in-jokes. It doesn't really make any sense that it worked out, but it was brilliant.

Coming up with a name for the band wasn't quite as easy. We went through so many different ideas. At one point I remember we were calling ourselves East of Eden and I don't even know why, so I'm glad it didn't stick! It was the very young and innocent Nathan Sykes who actually put forward The Wanted and we all took to it straight away. Now we just needed to find some fans!

I'm very proud of the movement that we created with our fans. At the time social media was a fairly new phenomenon. It definitely wasn't embraced by the music industry as standard the way it is now. These days, an artist pretty much won't get signed without having a social media following first, but back then it was totally new territory and one that the label wanted us to embrace. We went along with it and didn't really expect much, but it really opened our eyes once we started to see how we were connecting with people all over the country.

We used to upload a new YouTube video every week

called #WantedWednesday to give an insight into our lives and who we were as people. I loved making those videos, we'd get into all sorts of mischief and I think people really connected with us on a deeper level.

It was important to all of us that the fans felt like they were involved in The Wanted as much as possible. We'd host online competitions and would interact with them as much as we could, so we got a sense of who they were as well as them getting to know us. In the early days, we'd know all the names of our fans and it was really nice to see them at shows and get to talk to them.

To this day I'm thankful to all the people who supported us by following on those platforms from so early on: without them seeing some potential in us and investing in us as human beings first and foremost, we wouldn't have got the kick-start that we needed to launch our careers. All of that hard work we were putting in could well have led to nothing. We always wanted to make sure they knew how much we appreciated them.

Reflecting on those early days makes me realise that I always knew that there was hope. When I'd been sitting around in my mate's student flat smoking weed, I could never have anticipated where I'd find myself less than a year later. I think it's important to remember that we're always going to experience highs and lows throughout our lives and accepting this allows us to keep sight of the bigger picture.

Whenever we come across a bit of a slump, we can remind ourselves that it's only a matter of time before things start picking up again. Equally, moments of happiness or celebration are to be valued and experienced as fully present as possible. Because, whether good or bad, all moments pass. Life throws us all sorts of challenges which help us to become better, stronger and more resilient people.

'It felt as though it was meant for us, we just knew, "That is us, that is our record."'

7

'ALL TIME LOW'

Despite having made it into a band with a record deal, I'd still only ever seen recording studios in music videos and on TV. And the first time I actually set foot in one was to record our debut single, 'All Time Low'.

In pop music particularly, but other genres too, a lot of the songs that get released commercially are written and developed by songwriters and recorded in demo form, which are then shopped around to recording artists that they might resonate with. There was a time when that used to be looked down upon a lot by music fans and it was something that many artists would shy away from talking about, but nowadays it's more accepted as part of the collaborative process that leads to great pop songs. At the end of the day, matching a powerful and memorable song with the strongest performance, one that makes you feel something when you hear it, is what really results in the best pop music. And there are a lot of different ways to make that happen, which we'd learn while making our first album, *The Wanted*, in 2010.

Growing up listening to bands like Oasis and the Manics, I had held on to the belief that great bands write their own songs. But as I opened my mind to pop music, I began to see the other side of that debate. We would contribute writing to some of the songs later on in our career and we did a fair bit on that first album, but for those initial sessions our job was to work with songwriters to find tracks that would suit our voices, our identity as a band and set us up to be able to deliver the best performances. My passion was always singing first and foremost, so I was more than happy with that arrangement. Plus, when we found ourselves in front of people like Guy Chambers, who wrote 'Angels' for Robbie Williams, I would always be blown away – I felt honoured to be working with such iconic writers and we learned a lot from them.

While in the process of recording that first album, we'd listen to literally hundreds of demos along with our management and label before hitting on a gem that really resonated with us as individuals and what we wanted to stand for as a band. When we'd found something that everyone was happy with, we'd go to the studio and record our version of it. That's where we'd really make it our own and elevate the demo version to make it feel like The Wanted. 'All Time Low' is the perfect example of that process at its finest and it's a song that I fell in love with the moment I heard it.

The song was written by a guy called Ed Drewett and when we heard the demo version we knew immediately that it represented what we'd been looking for: this was the powerful opening statement that would establish The Wanted as a band. It felt as though it was meant for us, we just knew, 'That is us, that is our record.' Sometimes it feels like something is meant to be and that was one of those moments.

Recording 'All Time Low' was a truly incredible experience and one I'll never forget. Being in the studio felt so natural, from the moment I set foot in it. We each went in separately to record our parts on the track and I remember how surreal it felt, hearing my own voice playing back through the speakers. To this day, that's my favourite song that we ever made. It brings back so many memories and captures everything I loved about the music we made as The Wanted – the strings, the melodies, the beautiful lyrics.

Those initial sessions really felt like a magical time. We went to Copenhagen to record our next two songs, our second single 'Heart Vacancy', and a song that I love called 'Black Box', but that was eventually recorded by the *Australian Idol* winner, so we ended up not putting it out. I think when we finished up 'Heart Vacancy', we knew that we were onto something special. So we had two songs in the bag and both of them easily sounded like Top 40 material. That album depicted everything about us in that time, it was full of excitement. When I listen to it now it's such a nostalgic experience, it brings back a lot of memories.

We were up for doing anything we could to promote 'All Time Low' and I mean anything. We'd be up at the crack of dawn and in the back of a van, driving to perform school shows, under-18 clubs, anywhere that would have us. The schedule was brutal, but it always felt worth it when we were getting to meet our fans and making new ones along the way. We just loved performing together and we really believed in the songs that we had recorded. The hype was building around us and there was a lot of anticipation for us to release our first single.

When the week of the release came in October 2010, we kept going, with performances and signings all over the UK. I think we signed CDs for about 5,000 people at Westfield shopping centre in west London – we were there for hours, but we loved every minute of it. The support of the fans was more than enough, but soon we were being told that the single might make it into the Top 10 – we honestly couldn't believe it.

We had a lot of confidence in the record and the effort

we'd put in promoting it, so expected to do quite well. But on Sunday night when the charts were announced, none of us were expecting to hear that we'd reached No. 1. I cried like a baby. That's an achievement that nobody can ever take away from us. We had worked as a team, put in the work and it paid off – The Wanted will forever be UK No. 1 recording artists.

'She told one
of her mates,
"I love him".'

8

KELSEY

I first met the love of my life, Kelsey Hardwick, in December 2009, in the smoking area of Aura Mayfair, a nightclub in London's West End. I think she actually saw me first. She was with Pixie Lott, who happened to be her best mate from school. Apparently, Kelsey immediately told one of her mates, 'I'm in love with him.' It was literally love at first sight. We had tables next to each other inside the club, so I asked her name so I could look her up on Facebook. At the time I thought that was the cool thing to do, but she looked at me like I was mental!

'What do you do?' she asked.

'I'm in a band,' I replied.

'Okay, well, what's your band called?'

'We've not got a name yet.'

Her guy mates would pretend to be footballers when they went out in London, so she was sure I must be lying. Luckily for me, she told me her name anyway.

Later that night I was paralytically drunk, kissing this girl who I believed to be Kelsey. I soon discovered that I'd actually been with a totally different girl, who I had somehow managed to mistake for her. That gives you a bit of an idea of the state I was allowing myself to get into during those early days of living in London with the band. The next morning led to another case of mistaken identity. I sent a text to the only Kelsey that was in my phone; which turned out to be a guy I knew from Bolton!

I'm thankful to say that somehow, despite these embarrassing episodes, we did end up getting together. I managed to track her down on Facebook and she received my friend request while in the stock room of Dorothy Perkins, where she was working in the shoe department. A few days later we exchanged numbers.

It was coming towards the end of our first year as a band, and on our last day before we went home for a Christmas break, we were scheduled to record a performance for a kid's TV show where they had this terrible magician. We arrived at the studio with Jayne, and our bags packed for the holidays. During rehearsals, I couldn't believe how bad the magician was, I almost felt personally offended by his tricks! I felt like I had to take a stand. We couldn't be part of the performance.

'I'm not doing this,' I said. 'It's bullshit!'

'Okay, boys,' Jayne said. 'If you're going to make that decision, then I'll take the hit for this.'

She let us out through the fire escape and then had to go and break the news to everyone that we weren't going to do the show. The poor magician was actually a nice guy, but he was dreadful and I remember him having a really frantic energy. I knew that the show was going to be a car crash if we stayed. So we walked out before the recording even started.

Max and I went straight to Euston to take the train back up North. We got a couple of beers in at the station, and took our seats, ready to relax and chat shit for the three-hour journey back home.

We'd been sat there for about two minutes when I got a call.

'It's that girl, Kelsey, I met the other week in the nightclub,' I mouthed to Max.

I ended up staying on the phone until we pulled in at Manchester. It was the first time that I properly sat down and had a proper conversation with her, and I didn't want it to end. I gave Max a hug and said goodbye, then continued on to Bolton. Poor guy must have been bored shitless!

We texted each other all through the holidays, and I couldn't wait to meet up with her in January when we got back.

Kelsey was nineteen at the time, and I was twenty-one. She was recently out of college and had trained at Italia Conti Academy of Theatre Arts in London. She was juggling loads of different things; acting, dancing, teaching – always hustling.

I was always really impressed by all the things she'd be getting herself involved in. She knew what she wanted, and she was a go-getter like me. We had so much in common that people would say we were the boy and girl version of each other. We had such an instant connection, I knew that she was my person immediately.

I'm ashamed to say that this doesn't mean I treated her the way I should have straight away. In fact, I was quite shitty to her during our first year. I felt as though my commitment to being part of a rising boyband meant that I was unable be in a relationship. I thought that it might ruin my image. But at the same time, I couldn't keep away from her. I'd keep inviting her along to things, but I was afraid to make things official or call her my girlfriend. I regret acting like that. I had this idea of what a pop star was, and I was doing my best to live up to it, but I have to admit that I wasn't being true to myself.

We ended up separating, and we didn't talk for six

months. But I couldn't stop thinking about her. When it came to The Wanted playing our first headline show in London at the Hammersmith Apollo, I decided to see if I could win her back, and texted her an invite. I was surprised to see that she actually turned up, and for the entire show I sang to her. My eyes were glued to her the whole time.

Kelsey's friend, Ruth-Anne Cunningham, is a songwriter, and was with her at the show. She couldn't help but notice the chemistry between us in the room, even though Kelsey was pissed off with me, and how I was fixated on her the whole time. She ended up writing an amazing song about it called 'I'm Ready'.

Afterwards, Kelsey came backstage and I invited her to come out with the band and crew. She turned me down. I ended up crying to a random in the club toilets, telling them about how I'd lost the love of my life. It turned out that the guy whose shoulder I was, quite literally, crying on, was Kelsey's next-door neighbour, CJ. The next day he ended up giving Kelsey a lift to the train station and told her all about how devastated I was.

Shortly after all this, I was on holiday with Ali in Marbella. It was raining and I was having the worst time. I realised how stupid I was being and called Kelsey.

'I'm ready,' I said.

'What do you mean you're ready?' she asked.

'I'm ready to be with you now.'

'Okay, well, I might not be ready to be with you!'

Luckily, when we got back and met up, Kelsey was ready to be with me, and we got back together.

While we were living in the house in Wandsworth, Kelsey would be around all the time. Jay had a lizard that he used to let roam free, and it would scare the shit out of her. Sometimes, if I'd been out working for the day, I would get home to find her locked in my bedroom. She'd be there for the whole day because she was terrified of the lizard.

We ended up moving in to a flat in Battersea together, and it was absolutely incredible. I loved that place, it was costing me an arm and a leg, but it was the absolute bollocks! We would always have the best parties there and it was right on the Thames.

For those first few years we probably spent more time in central London nightclubs than our home, being wild youths. But at least this time we were definitely together, there was no mistake about it. We used to go to the local pub, The Magic Garden, all of the time, and then we'd go out clubbing where we would be plied with free alcohol.

The next morning we'd have to face the aftermath in the form of wild paparazzi photos. I don't think there was ever a nice picture of us! There we'd be, staggering out of some club in the early hours, middle fingers up to the cameras like the rockstars we clearly thought we were.

The press would be harsh on Kelsey at times, without thinking about her feelings as a 21-year-old woman. But she was always so strong and positive that she saw straight through their bullshit and didn't let it get to her.

I just thought she was the most amazing human on the planet anyway, so I would never put her down and did my best to make sure that none of the media stuff would affect her.

Despite my initial concerns about being a pop star in a relationship, The Wanted fans really embraced Kelsey, which was lovely. I think she's a great role model who a lot of them can really relate to.

Kelsey's dad left when she was 11, and her mum Diane set an incredible example for her, by always remaining positive throughout her life. I think that's what's made her such an uplifting person to be around; she just doesn't dwell on things. Whatever it is that we're faced with, she will always look for a way to deal with it. That's always been something I've really valued.

She never really gave me a hard time about being in the band, and I know that at times, particularly at the height of our fame, it could have been difficult for her, but Kelsey just doesn't overthink anything. She keeps herself rooted in the reality of what is happening in the moment, and what she is able to control, and then she gets on with it.

She's independent and has her own fun. When I was away with the boys, she would be doing her own thing. I think we have a very secure relationship; she always knew that she was my number one, and I knew I was hers.

When people meet us as a couple, I think she's the more confident one, which often surprises people. At first, I was a ball of energy, but I think getting used to fame has forced me to withdraw a little bit. I'm more sensitive and emotional than her, while she's got a tougher exterior and is probably more resilient than me.

I think that us meeting when we did helped us to stay grounded. We've remained the people that we always were. If I ever did get a bit carried away, she would tell me to shut up!

She's my guardian angel. She's my rock. Kelsey never treated me as famous, and I loved that about her and our relationship. What we have is so strong, it's something that people spend a lifetime searching for, and we're lucky that we found it so early.

'The best way to live is in the here and now.'

9

THE MUSIC
INDUSTRY

Amazing as those early months of being in the band were, I have to admit that they weren't without difficulty. It's easy to erase the sides of life that were more difficult and look at the past with rose-tinted glasses but, being honest, I started to understand very quickly that the music business is fucking controlling. While I was always appreciative of the opportunity we'd been given, on the first album campaign we were dictated to about every aspect of our lives. That's not to say that was always a bad thing – as I've said already, I love 'All Time Low' to this day – and I think that was an example of the pop music machine working at its best. But sometimes it was difficult for me to stomach.

As the oldest in the group (I beat Max by a couple of months), I felt protective towards the rest of the boys and developed a father figure role very early on. I thought it was my responsibility to make sure that we weren't being taken advantage of. For the most part we just had to swallow the pill and get on with it – we didn't really have much power at that point and the option to continue with what we were doing far outweighed going back to sleeping on couches.

I think that my leadership role within the group was also fuelled by my dedication towards success for all of us. I've always been driven once I set my mind to something. I'll admit that I'm quite partial to a lie-in, but as long as I can get my beauty sleep, when I like something and I'm focused on it, I want everyone around me to approach it with the same attitude. At times I would feel as though the others were getting a bit lazy and that would annoy me, given the amount of work it had taken us all to get to where we were. I'd try to inspire them by reminding them of how far we'd come since the days of dragging ourselves back and forwards to auditions – I was determined not to lose what we'd gained by becoming complacent.

You can get lost in this industry very easily, but I knew it was important to stay humble and keep a level head. I think it's been advantageous to me that I've stayed that way throughout my career as it's helped me to keep up some great relationships with record executives and artists alike. However, it was always in my mind that eventually I would like to get to the point where I could have more autonomy over my own career; that I'd learn as much as I could from the situation I was in, lead the boys as best I could and eventually we'd be able to do things on our terms. I feel like this time around, with our reunion, the release of *Most Wanted: The Greatest Hits* and the tour, we've finally been able to reach that goal. It's such a great feeling after all of these years to have achieved that and I'm really proud of how far we've come. To say that we've proved ourselves to the industry at this stage is a massive understatement and to be able to be more creative and take things into our own hands this time around is extremely rewarding.

Sometimes when I think back to those early days I realise that I didn't appreciate a lot of those moments that came with being young and finding success. Life was hurtling along at such a rate that it wasn't until much later in life that I was able to slow down and understand what we had managed to create. If you ever have an experience like I did, I'd urge you to try and learn to take things in while they're happening to you: the best way to live is in the here and now.

I think that really hit me when JLS split up in 2013. We were still active and had always seen them as being slightly ahead of us on their trajectory as a boy band. Following them was a bit of a learning curve. I could see how slick and controlled their project looked, while at times being in the middle of ours felt like a bit of a mess. When they announced that they were breaking up, it made me realise that what we were doing could all disappear in a second. It's important just to take things in and appreciate them while they're happening.

I suppose that was also a lesson in not looking at others and assuming that they're doing better than you, just because of how things look on the outside. I think most of us are guilty of looking at someone's Instagram feed at one point or another, taking in all of the amazing things they're doing and feeling like we're inferior. But just because someone is showing all of their highlights to the world on social media doesn't mean that they're not dealing with other difficulties behind closed doors. It's best that we focus on ourselves and strive to be the best versions of ourselves.

We were definitely guilty of getting swept up in comparison when we had a rivalry with One Direction. I believe it might have started with a quote in the media that had been taken out of context. We actually were really interested in them and even played their songs and sang along. There was never any malice towards them. The majority of the drama happened over Twitter, embarrassingly, with names thrown back and forwards from both camps. As much as they smashed it, we didn't really care, because we were doing well and that was it. We looked at them as a crazy phenomenon, and what they were doing was actually really cool. But you're only the centre of your own universe, so we only really saw our fans, our gigs, our record sales, our tour bus. We never necessarily felt like part of this celebrity – we felt like we were the normal ones looking at all of these other people doing crazy stuff, and sometimes we crossed paths.

Their fans hated us and our fans hated them. The media loved the whole thing of course, but looking back, it was all quite pathetic really. Everything got blown out of proportion and when you're in that bubble, you just go with it, even if you might not necessarily feel that way. Everybody got carried away with themselves. It is what it is. Certain situations happen sometimes that are out of your control. It was all part of being caught up in the hype of the music industry.

'We were
having the time
of our lives.'

10

I COULD'VE SHOWN YOU AMERICA

I was with Kelsey in our flat in Battersea on 10 January 2010, when I answered the call that would begin a new chapter for the band.

'Listen, we need you in America tomorrow.' It was the A&R from our label Geffen Records. 'We need you on a flight because you've got some promo to do.'

Our latest single 'Glad You Came', which was already a UK No. 1, had started connecting at radio in the US and they wanted us out there in the market to push it. By that same time the next day I was in New York with the boys and we were preparing to perform a one-off showcase for some fans and industry people who had been invited down by the label.

We ended up staying out there for three months to promote the record and in many ways it was like starting out all over again. It was a very exciting time. We were in a new country and we had to build a new fanbase out there, but we'd done it all before and had the support of the UK fans behind us, so we were up for the challenge.

I fell in love with life on the road, touring all over America on a bus with my mates, all of us in our twenties: doing all of the radio shows, meeting fans, performing, going to bed and then waking up in another new city. We were having the time of our lives.

I particularly liked spending time in Los Angeles, which was lucky really, because we ended up being over there a lot. Geffen put us up at this luxury five-star hotel in West Hollywood called The Mondrian, which for a Bolton boy like myself felt way too posh. If you want a coffee, you have to phone down and get some fancy concoction that costs $20! Needless to say, I ended up spending most of my time at the bar across the street instead. The Saddle Ranch became my second home – it came alive after dark and there was a bucking bronco. If you walked into that bar any night that The Wanted were in town, the chances are you'd see me, Max and Jay in there – Nathan sadly was too young at the time and Siva was much too refined, he would be in his room reading a book!

During that trip we ended up with the opportunity to perform 'Glad You Came' on *American Idol*, which was incredible. The energy was amazing and there were loads of fans in the audience, which was still surprising to us whenever we weren't in the UK. The judging panel on the show was Jennifer Lopez, Steven Tyler and Randy Jackson, who were all really nice. We were even invited to celebrate J.Lo's birthday party after the show.

The level of what fame could be in America was so much bigger, so although we'd become one of the biggest boy bands in the UK, it took some readjustment to process everything that was happening for us out there. Aside from the 19-hour bus trips, we were having the chance to live relatively normal lives again – we could walk into a bar and nobody would look twice at us. Which was quite nice actually. But then we would experience these incredible highs that felt totally surreal. Sitting around a table drinking shots with J.Lo was definitely the latter – I had to pinch myself to make sure that it wasn't all in my imagination. The next day we woke up to all of these American news shows reporting on us as these 'adorable Brits' who were taking on America, peppered with selfies of us with J.Lo.

One of the American promotion trips that I remember most fondly was when Ed Sheeran joined us on our tour bus. Our first ever tour manager, Mark Friend, went to work for Ed so we've always been friends. Ed was starting out in America at the same time as us, and since you have to do these long drives across the country and he was on the same route, it made sense for him to come along with us. You'd go to bed in one US state after enjoying a day of sun and wake up driving through snow. The vastness of that country is unlike anything I'd ever experienced in my life.

There was a bit of an uproar on the bus one night when Ed got a call to say 'The A Team' had been nominated for Song of the Year at the Grammys.

'What the fuck!?!' I piped up, laughing. 'How the fuck have you got that?'

'Glad You Came' was out at the time too, and was doing much better in the charts. We continued to lovingly rip him, before all getting rat-arsed to celebrate.

I was a massive fan of Ed and we've always run into each other over the years and had a great relationship. He's an amazing artist but an even better person. He's one of those exceptions to the rule, an idol who you really should meet.

It's weird, really, how much our and Ed's professional lives have crossed. As well as sharing tour managers, our security guy, Kevin Myers – or Big Kev, as he's affectionately known – who was with us from the beginning went on to work for Ed when we called it a day. You will always see Big Kev in the papers and on the telly, right by Ed's side, just as he was for us. We always joke that Kev is the most successful member of The Wanted but, despite the gruff exterior, he's a lovely guy. Kev and our long-suffering tour manager Martin were like our second dads for all those years, and I've got so much to be grateful to them for.

We had other guests hop on The Wanted tour bus as well. There was even a stint where Lindsay Lohan was with us. During one particular episode she'd come to see us warming up for Justin Bieber at Madison Square Garden in New York, then I went along with Jay and Max to meet her for a drink afterwards at Club Avenue in Manhattan. Somehow Lindsay ended up in an altercation with a woman at the club and got herself arrested for it. She spent that night in a jail cell. The next morning, Jay, Max and I decided to emerge from our hotel wearing 'Free Lindsay' T-shirts that we'd made with felt-tip pens – I think Jay might even have worn his for our show that night. Naturally the press loved it and decided to make Max the reason that Lindsay was fighting in the first place. It all added to the growing image of us in America as this boy band who had come over from Britain and weren't afraid of a bit of controversy.

One afternoon we were on our way to film our US late-night debut on the comedienne Chelsea Handler's show, *Chelsea Lately*, when we were stopped by a guy whose 11-year-old daughter wanted an autograph. Her name was Mackenzie and she was super excited to see us. At the time that was a fairly normal experience for us, even in America, so we obliged and then got on with what we had to do.

When we left after a full afternoon of filming, the dad was still outside, but this time he was completely panicked. It filled me with dread when I heard him say that Mackenzie had gone missing. I could feel it in the pit of my stomach, I felt truly awful for him.

Things quickly went from bad to worse when he began to blame us for her disappearance, but we were urged to continue on, as the security at the venue assisted the father and offered to help. Everyone was pretty shaken up and we were all fairly quiet on the drive back to the hotel. I couldn't stop worrying about her – I just hoped that there had been some kind of misunderstanding and she'd been found.

All of a sudden, we heard police sirens behind us.

'Aww crap,' said our driver. 'Sorry, fellas, we gotta pull over.'

We pulled off into a parking lot and these two mountainous police officers approached the van.

'Get out! Put your hands up and get against the wall.'

It was like something that you'd see in a film, but when it's your reality, it's a nightmare. My thoughts were racing. The five of us, along with our driver, security guy and tour manager stood in the afternoon heat, our hands pushed into the concrete wall of a petrol station. This was a challenge I'd never anticipated having to deal with.

After some time, they must have realised we weren't much of a threat and let us sit down.

'You don't know why we pulled you over?' they asked, before addressing me directly. 'What about you, my man?'

'I think it's because we weren't wearing seat belts?' I blurted out.

One of the cops pulled me aside.

'You have no idea why you're here, do you?' he asked.

'I honestly couldn't tell you,' I said, suddenly realising that the police helicopter circling above was linked to this whole ordeal.

'We have a missing girl,' said the officer.

I noticed Mackenzie's dad, approaching from another police car that had just pulled up. And this time, rather than panicking like before, he was furious.

'This is The Wanted guys, I know exactly who they are,' he said, pointing to the rest of the band, still sitting in line along the wall.

'If we don't find this girl, you're in big trouble,' the cop told me.

'Let me take a look in the back of the car,' said his partner, walking over to our van.

Obviously, I expected it to be just full of our bags, but when he pulled open the back doors, sure enough, Mackenzie wandered out. I didn't know what the fuck was going on. She must have stowed herself away while our driver was taking a call or something. But it didn't look good for us. I was partly angry, relieved that Mackenzie had been found, but mostly terrified about what was going to happen next. The dad was still extremely pissed off, but he began to soften as she ran up to him and he lifted her into his arms.

'What are you doing inside this van?' he asked.

'They … they took me,' she responded.

I just felt helpless – I didn't know what was going to happen to us and I started to cry.

'Why is she in your van?' the cop asked me, repeatedly. 'Tell me how she got in the van.'

'I couldn't honestly tell you, I really couldn't.'

It was all I could muster up. I was totally overwhelmed.

'I can't understand a word you're saying right now. Do the best you can to lose the accent,' the officer demanded. 'You think you're better than us, don't you?'

I saw his colleagues start to cuff the other boys.

'Honestly, I wouldn't even think about doing something like that, I really wouldn't.'

'Lie down on your stomach.'

I knew they weren't playing around, I could see most of the other lads were cuffed at this stage and so I did what I was told. I wished I was back at home in London, I just felt like I had no control over the situation and no idea what was going to happen to us. You see so much in films about the US legal system and prisons. Fuck knew what was going to happen if they really thought we'd kidnapped this kid.

The dad started to accuse Nathan of inviting her on

tour with us, while we were signing autographs for her, and Nathan began to get frustrated. We were moved over to join the rest of the boys, cuffed against the wall.

'Mackenzie, I'm going to ask you one last time, this is real serious, okay?'

The cop was behind us, speaking calmly and firmly, loud enough so that we could all hear.

'People will go to jail. I need to know, how did you get in the van, Mackenzie?'

'These guys took me,' she confirmed.

I couldn't believe what I was hearing.

'I want to press charges,' demanded her dad.

I was terrified.

The cop asked us to turn around and as we did, the horror flooded from my body, replaced with relief and laughter. US rapper Tyler, the Creator and an entire film crew were running at us; his expression was full of mischief – he was laughing his head off.

'You got *Punk'd*!'

Suddenly I was so full of energy and relief that I started sprinting around the parking lot. I couldn't believe they'd got us. I'd watched celebrities getting pranked on the TV show *Punk'd* for years and never once thought that I'd ever be gullible enough to get caught. In some ways I never suspected it because I didn't even realise that we were at that level yet. In hindsight, it's one of the funniest things that happened to us during our whole career – they definitely got me, but in the moment it was so realistic that I was bricking it the entire time. I was having visions of the rest of my life in a jail cell that day and instead here we were on one of the biggest TV shows in America with one of the most exciting new rappers, who would go on to become a global icon.

While our travels in America definitely provided us with some career highlights, at times we found it difficult to connect with how different the entertainment industry over there could be. We certainly got ourselves lost in translation a few times, especially me as a no-nonsense Northerner. My directness got me in trouble amid the pretentious celebrity lifestyle of Los Angeles.

While promoting 'Chasing The Sun', we went to perform it on *The Voice* over there in April 2012. The judges for the US version were Christina Aguilera, CeeLo Green, Adam Levine and Blake Shelton. We were excited to meet Christina and who wouldn't be? She's an icon! But we were quite disappointed by the fact that she just completely ignored us and wouldn't interact whatsoever. I always want to treat people as human beings, no matter who I'm dealing with. I've been raised to treat people with good manners and so I think we left with a bit of a bad taste in our mouths – it felt like she had no respect for us.

Shortly afterwards we had an interview with a New York radio station called 92.3 NOW FM and they asked us questions about Christina. You quickly get used to having to answer questions about other celebrities or artists who are bigger than you when you're coming up as a pop act, or in this case, starting afresh in a new territory. The press are just looking for a headline and what better way than to ask questions about other famous people? It's all part of the game and I was generally quite comfortable with it, but perhaps that day I was *too* comfortable and so I shared my exact feeling at that time.

'She's a total bitch,' I told them, a quote I'm ashamed to say was plastered all over the news for the next few days. 'She might not be a bitch in real life, but to us, she was a total bitch. She just sat there and didn't speak to us. Wouldn't even look at us.'

The rest of the boys were more diplomatic in their answers and they were right to be. I don't think being disrespectful to her just because I'd felt disrespected myself was ever going to result in anything good. I'll just have to chalk it to being young, less self-aware and out of my comfort zone in a different country. The music industry can push you to be someone you don't want to be very easily. I'm just lucky that when things did get out of hand I was always able to humble myself and remember where I'd come from. Calling her that wasn't acceptable and I knew that as soon as I'd said it. That's not how I was raised. The next day, when a reporter from TMZ caught us outside of The Mondrian, I used the opportunity to apologise.

A week later came another controversy when Siva gave an interview to another New York radio station, Fresh FM, and told a story about a strange experience we'd had with Britney Spears when we were supporting her at Manchester's M.E.N Arena during the UK leg of her *Femme Fatale* tour in November 2011.

We'd been with our tour manager trying to get some Wi-Fi backstage when suddenly her security team approached us and asked that we all face the wall so that she could walk past without us looking at her. This felt totally bizarre and again disrespectful, so I guess it stuck with all of us and Siva shared it publicly during that interview. Again, it caught on with the wider press, particularly off the back of my comments about Christina. Britney's team responded, denying the story was true and highlighting the fact that we'd had problems with two iconic pop women in the past week.

Reflecting on it now, I think that perhaps I was a little bit insecure as I tried to come to terms with the mammoth task of breaking America. I got swept up in the hype, but sometimes things didn't play out quite as I'd imagined them and then I think that caused me to lash out a bit. I've learned that it's important not to hold on to expectations of events or even people. If I leave space for different outcomes, then

I'm usually much more positive about the results. Often setting expectations leads to disappointment, but keeping an open mind allows us to accept and enjoy the reality and often leads us to surprise ourselves.

Although I wasn't aware of it at the time, it was probably quite difficult to process the difference of being a huge act at home and then working to build ourselves from the ground up in the States. It was a very exciting time and I loved it, but there was still a lot for us to learn. We were used to being personable and down-to-earth with everyone we met so at times when that wasn't reciprocated, I jumped to conclusions. It's important to consider other angles when communicating with people and not judge them too harshly. Christina might have just been having a bad day, but because that was the day I met her, I allowed my disappointment to make a judgement about her. And then to make matters worse, I shared it on a public platform.

I suppose the downside to the whole thing about being in the States was that there were a lot of late nights, poor nutrition and, overall, it wasn't the healthiest way to live. We ate a lot of garage sandwiches and crisps. But, aside from that and all of the fun we were having, the trip was a massive success and we managed to get

'Glad You Came' to No. 3 on the US Billboard charts, which was pretty unbelievable.

Undoubtedly the most memorable part of the whole trip was meeting Michelle Obama. Every year at the White House, there is an event called the Easter Egg Roll, it's hosted on the South Lawn and as part of it they have an artist perform. In 2013 we had the honour of being invited to play. I remember feeling very privileged and thinking to myself, *How did a kid from Bolton end up being invited to the White House, to meet the First Lady?* It was mind-boggling!

As well as the performance, part of the tradition is 'Story Time'. We were asked to read a 1940s children's book called *Caps for Sale* by Esphyr Slobodkina to kids who were gathered on this beautiful green lawn in the White House gardens. We were supposed to take it in turns reading a page, passing the book along. It turned out to be the most ridiculous ten minutes of our lives.

The wind was blowing and making all sorts of noises through the microphones, but we just needed to pull it together and do our best to be nice British (and Irish) boys reading to the children. We were doing a decent job until we reached this part in the book that kept repeating the line, 'he pulled off his cap.' The innuendo was too much for us. Being admittedly immature, we couldn't stop laughing as we struggled to reach the end of the story.

At one point Max pretended he was struggling with

his eyesight so that he could pass the book over to me. I tried to save us by changing the phrase to 'took off his cap', handing the book back along the line, hoping Max would do the same. But he didn't get my hint. I don't think anyone other than us had a clue why we were all pissing ourselves laughing, and we didn't even finish the story.

'We're not the best readers,' I said, as we got up and made a swift exit. 'I apologise.'

That video remains on the Obama White House YouTube page to this day, where it has over 40,000 views!

Afterwards, we had the honour of being led on a tour of the White House by Michelle Obama and a member of the Secret Service, who took us around the entire house – except the very top floor where her and Barack's bedroom was.

'Nobody goes up there except me and my husband,' she said.

We went to the Oval Office, the kitchen, the bowling alley that they just have for their family, the library and a room where they still have a load of stacked burnt chairs.

'This is from when the British attacked the White House 200 years ago,' Michelle explained.

'Sorry!' we all responded in unison!

There was a secret toilet in the library and we all gathered in there and recorded a video of us singing the 'Sitting on the toilet' meme that was going around at the time. We never posted it!

It was an unbelievable experience. Our day-to-day manager at the time, Nano Tissera, was so proud of us for being there and brought his mum along. He had toured with all sorts of big names over the years and was usually not impressed by much. They were so overwhelmed. Our team there was probably freaking out more than us.

We even ended up meeting Michelle again a couple of months later, at the US Open at Arthur Ashe Stadium in New York.

'We're so proud of you,' she said with a warm smile.

There's no way we thought that she would have remembered who we were, we assumed we'd be long out of her mind. She'd been watching us since our visit and followed how much we'd grown. We couldn't believe she'd said she was proud of us. It was such a kind comment and so meaningful for us to hear.

It took some time for us to even realise how crazy it was. I think we were so swept up in the whirlwind of everything that was happening to us in America, that even the surreal had started to seem normal. If somebody called me today to invite me to wander around the White House with Michelle Obama I don't think I'd be able to believe it. When opportunities like that present themselves, you just have to take them and enjoy the moments.

One of our biggest achievements during our time in America had to be when we won the People's Choice Award for Favourite Breakthrough Artist, which was massive for us. When we found out that we'd been nominated we pledged that if we won, we would dedicate a song to Ellen Degeneres for taking a risk by having us on her show and giving us our first big break on US television. We sang 'Afternoon Delight', a ridiculously suggestive song by Starland Vocal Band that we knew from the film *Anchorman*, in harmony, as part of our acceptance speech. I didn't actually think we were going to win, so it didn't seem likely that we would have to do it.

But when we did end up at the Nokia Theatre in Los Angeles, being declared winners, we had to commit. Jay kicked things off and we all joined in. The crowd loved it, and Ellen was so surprised that she had us on her show again a couple of days later, where she called our acceptance speech her favourite moment of the show! It was our first major international award and we were up against One Direction who, despite our rivalry, I have to admit were always outdoing us at the awards. We used to joke about the fact that we were nominated for a load of big awards but they would always beat us to it.

Winning that People's Choice award felt like a moment of acceptance. We never hunted awards, one was good enough for us, and that win felt really special. It's voted for by the American public, so it felt like a real moment of acceptance for us in the States.

We celebrated that night by going to a brilliantly named upmarket Mexican place called Pink Taco on Sunset

Boulevard. Our whole team was with us and it wasn't too far away from The Saddle Ranch, so afterwards we paraded up the street with our award to finish the night at what had become our favourite spot in the whole of Los Angeles.

In the morning, none of us could remember where we had put the award. We never did find it.

'When we lose something that is important to us, we also gain the space and time for something new and different to blossom.'

11

HIATUS

We enjoyed about a year of global success off the back of that unforgettable trip, by the end of which we'd sold an astounding 12 million records worldwide. That would have been unthinkable to any of us when we started out as an unnamed band. We were a phenomenal success story and I thought we had a lot further to go, but that all came to an abrupt halt in 2013, when we were told the label wanted us to take a break.

It started to become clear that we all had different goals and maybe our work as The Wanted had run its course. After the highs that had come with success in America, a lot of our obligations began to feel like work. Beforehand, they'd mostly felt like exciting opportunities and things we'd have probably wanted to do even if nobody was paying us for it. I think that's the best way to live life – if you're able to find something to do that fulfils you at an emotional level, not just financially. Once everything feels like a chore, it's a good time to start thinking about making a change. That being said, I still don't feel as though I was part of the decision for us to break up, that decision was made for me. It felt horrendous at the time. The band had been our lives for the past five years and suddenly it was being snatched away from us. I remember going home thinking, *That's the end?*

Perhaps it wasn't such a bad thing after all.

When you travel the world for five years it takes its toll. At that point we were all physically and mentally exhausted, so in some ways it was a blessing in disguise. It was like being with your four brothers every single day. We love each other, but there's only so much you can take! It was nice to be able to separate things a little bit; it was good to be out of that whirlwind of being in a band, doing promo and constantly touring. Suddenly I had a lot of time on my hands, which I could use for self-development.

It was nice to have some time to wind down and spend some time with Kelsey. We got a dog and a mortgage, and it was good to spend some time away from the limelight. We had the time we needed to build a family – which has been by far the most rewarding part of my life so far.

While pop music had played such a big part of my life during my time with The Wanted, I always wanted to explore my passion for dance music and was keen to start producing and DJing. I started teaching myself how to programme beats using music software like Logic Pro in my home studio.

I also got the opportunity to do things that I could never have done while we were active in the band, like appearing on the BBC's *Celebrity MasterChef* – which, as a foodie, had been a lifelong ambition of mine. I managed to do really well on that and despite cutting my finger and being unable to complete a round that involved making pasties and sausage rolls, I made it through to the semi-finals.

I actually turned down appearing on the Channel 4 skiing show *The Jump* originally, because I was worried it would open me up to a lot of criticism and I felt like being on a reality TV show was completely different to being in music. I agreed to train with the rest of the celebrities as a stand-in, assuming I wouldn't be needed and that I might just get to have fun learning to ski in Austria. But when the *Holby City* actress Tina Hobley fell on her arm during practice and dislocated her elbow, I ended up having to compete. In the end I had a great time and managed to come in third place.

Having some time away from the band reminded me that when we lose something that is important to us, like a job or a relationship, we also gain the space and time for something new and different to blossom. I think I got so caught up in my career with the band that I had begun to believe it was the only thing that I could have success in. But there is so much more out there to explore in life, and with loss always comes new opportunities.

It was hard to step away, but I always said that you had to be realistic and that everything has a shelf life. We'd officially called our time apart a 'hiatus', which obviously keeps things open for the possibility that we'd come back together some day. So, whenever I was asked about it I'd always say things like 'Never say never'. I think a part of me was hanging on and hoping that one day we'd perform together again.

Nothing in life is ever permanent: as final as I thought the breakup with The Wanted felt at the time, there would always be the opportunity for us to reconnect in the future.

'Kelsey helps me to keep a positive mental attitude, no matter what I'm facing in life.'

12

MARRIAGE

Marriage has always meant a lot to me. I think that the example set by my parents really instilled me with a strong family bond that respected and valued the idea of people making such a lifelong commitment to one another.

Looking back, at first, it meant so much to me that I was scared of it. When Kelsey and I were a bit younger and we would talk about it, she would say that she wanted to be married by the age of twenty-five, which seemed terrifying. But I always knew that marriage was something that I wanted eventually.

I have to admit that I am probably the more romantic

out of the two of us. There was a date we went on during our days living in Battersea where we went on a cruise down the Thames. I'd cut out fifty love hearts and written a reason why I loved Kelsey on each one. Then I lit a load of candles and left them in the flat while we were away. Although she loved the sentiment, Kelsey couldn't help but point out that my gesture could potentially have been quite dangerous.

In 2016, I was away in Austria for six weeks filming *The Jump*. About a week after I got back, we had a party with everyone from the show, and everyone but Kelsey was aware of my plan to propose to her the following day. Even so, we allowed Kelsey to reach the point of drunkenness where she was throwing up, and to be honest the rest of us probably weren't that far behind her.

The morning after, the two of us took a trip to Chewton Glen in Hampshire, where I'd booked a spectacular lodge for us to stay. We'd been together for six years by this point and it felt like the right time to begin the next chapter in our journey together.

I spent months planning the trip, but naturally some aspects took a little longer than I'd intended. The ring arrived very close to my planned proposal date, and I think I'd probably caused a fair bit of anxiety to her family in how last minute it was.

Kelsey followed the trail of roses I'd arranged which guided her to the TV, where a montage of photographs recalled some of our best moments together, and I was down on one knee, in tears! I couldn't get my words out. I was so overcome with emotion.

Once I did manage to pop the question, she said yes, and then we were joined by our families, who I'd arranged to join us as a surprise. It went perfectly!

A Parker wedding would require a lot of partying, so we needed to find the perfect venue. We didn't want to be told what to do by the venue staff, we wanted a place where there would be some freedom.

Kelsey was interviewing someone to come and work at her performing arts school, K2K Stars, when she happened to mention that she was looking at wedding venues. They recommended looking into Ridge Farm, a 16th century farmhouse on the Surrey-Sussex border.

We went to have a look, and it felt perfect the minute we set foot in it. It's actually an old recording studio where artists like Oasis, Ozzy Osbourne and Queen have recorded. There's even a photo of Freddie Mercury sitting out on the patio. When we saw that, we were like, 'This is the venue for us.' There were no rules, you could stay up as late as you wanted and get married anywhere on the grounds.

Our wedding took place on 14 July 2018. Ridge Farm

was packed out with our friends and family who arrived on the Friday night and stayed until the Sunday. It was a full weekend of non-stop partying and surprises.

Our first dance was to the song 'I'm Ready', which had been written by our friend Ruth-Anne about the night I invited Kelsey to The Wanted's first headline show, and spent the entire performance fixated on her.

I had been planning a surprise performance for Kelsey with all of the kids from K2K Stars, and we'd been rehearsing it weekly while she was teaching at another dance school on Fridays. I sang 'Heart Vacancy' with Max and Jay, then the kids all came out when we got to the chorus. Kelsey's face was priceless.

She had also been secretly working on a performance of Beyoncé's 'Crazy In Love' with some of her mates, and her aunty Julie did an incredible job of coordinating the whole weekend.

I'm thankful that we have always been surrounded by people who have helped us to create such special moments. The weekend was a non-stop party from start to finish, and the wedding day itself was truly one of the best days of my life.

I love the fact that we're married. At times I definitely had my concerns about how huge of a commitment it seemed to be, but marrying Kelsey is a decision that I've never looked back on. I remember there was a time when I used to say that I couldn't wear a ring, because it felt weird having something on my finger. She ended up saying that if I wouldn't wear a ring, then she wouldn't marry me. Now, when I look at my finger, that symbol of our marriage feels so powerful. I wouldn't be half the man that I am now without Mrs Kelsey Parker by my side.

'Being a father
is easily the most
rewarding part of
my life so far.'

13

AURELIA

Anyone who is a parent understands the unimaginable life change that comes with that role. To be honest, fatherhood was never something that I imagined was on the agenda for me but when we found out a couple of years ago that Kelsey was pregnant, I felt like the proudest man in the world.

Kelsey and I have always believed in the importance of having a positive mindset to get through the challenging aspects of life and so with our first child on the way, we decided to go to hypnobirthing classes.

Hypnobirthing is a practice that involves visualisation and mindfulness that helps you to form a connection with your unborn baby and is supposed to help the mother to manage pain naturally during labour. I wanted to be as involved as I could and it was encouraged for fathers to join the classes too, which I really enjoyed. Apart from breathing exercises, they taught you about meditation and how to create a bubble or 'happy place' that you can access during times of stress.

We were asked to write down our biggest fear about childbirth and I did give Kelsey a bit of a shock when she realised mine was that she might die. It probably wasn't the most tactful thing for me to write down, but I was being honest. She hadn't even considered the possibility, which is perhaps a better way to be in that situation. To this day she'll call me 'Negative Nancy' to help me catch when I'm looking at something in a glass-half-empty sort of way. Her positivity helps lift me back up and channels my more optimistic side.

Hypnobirthing was actually really helpful even beyond childbirth. It's all about asking questions and taking owner-ship of how you want to do things. If you were going to buy a house then you would ask questions about it, you wouldn't just stand there and have the estate agent dictate everything to you. Giving birth is even more personal and so it's important that you ask the questions that will allow you to do it in a way that works for you and your partner. I think that process trained Kelsey and me to be more curious about the options on offer and to explore all the alternatives, rather than just take what the first person hands to us.

AURELIA

It was the hottest day of the year, 30 June 2019, when our daughter Aurelia Rose (Aurelia meaning 'The Golden One', which she is, obviously) was born. I'm going to be honest when I say that even after the lessons, I wasn't ready to witness childbirth. I was a complete mess. The experience of being there for the birth was honestly horrific – it really drained Kelsey of everything she's got. All the goodness that Kelsey had, Aurelia took from her. Kelsey suffered really badly from pre-eclampsia, a condition that can affect pregnant women during the second half of pregnancy. It can cause things like headaches, vomiting, high blood pressure and swelling, and can lead to serious complications if it isn't taken care of. We didn't realise how poorly she was with it and she was swelling for six weeks before the birth – it got so bad that I used to call her 'Princess Fiona' from *Shrek*!

I was an emotional wreck the whole time. All I could bring myself to do was to go home and get all these fans to try and cool her down – the hospital room was full of them. Kelsey's mum Diane arrived to help us and I was in tears. I thought I'd overheard them saying that she was being taken in for an emergency C-section, which she'd repeatedly told me she didn't want, and I felt awful about it. Luckily when we got into theatre they did manage to get her to get Aurelia out with forceps. It was brutal to watch, truly horrendous.

Kelsey was trying her best to put into practice all of the

techniques that we had learned through hypnobirthing and had no pain relief, just gas and air, so she did amazingly well. I definitely didn't manage to get to my happy place while all of that was going on, I could hardly breathe. It was so difficult to see Kelsey there, struggling so badly, and there was nothing I could do to help her.

I remember walking out of the toilets and seeing her high on the gas and air, slurring at me.

'What are you crying for? I'm the one going through this! Get over here and get on this gas with me!'

I burst into laughter. Somehow no matter what happens, Kelsey manages to find the humour in a situation.

Once Aurelia was born, she was crying non-stop.

Is this fucking normal? I wondered to myself. *Why's she crying?*

I gave Aurelia a formula bottle to calm her down, which was a massive mistake. I didn't know that giving it to her immediately after her birth could have potentially disrupted Kelsey's plans of breastfeeding. Saying Kelsey was furious is an understatement, but luckily she was able to go on with breastfeeding.

The newborn phase was fucking hard work and definitely more for Kelsey than me, but being a father is easily the most rewarding part of my life so far. Your whole world gets turned upside down. As soon as I looked into Aurelia's eyes, I knew that I was going to be completely obsessive as a dad. I Googled everything, just wanting to make sure she was safe and protected. If she started crying, I would drive her around the M25 to try and help her go to sleep. At the time, it felt like she was this little thing who was just so reliant on us to help her survive, but I think I massively underestimated just how smart and intuitive children are. It's been a mind-blowing experience. It's truly beautiful being her dad.

Part Two

'I needed to be able to live with hope.'

14

DIAGNOSIS

After spending months in lockdown, in August 2020 Kelsey and I decided it was time for a break so we took Aurelia for a couple of weeks holiday in Norfolk with Kelsey's family. As we were getting ready to leave, packing up the car, locking the front door, I never imagined how much my life would change before I'd cross that doorstep again.

I hadn't been feeling quite right around that time, but I couldn't put my finger on what the issue was. Something strange had happened a few weeks prior. It's quite difficult to explain because whatever it was, I don't remember it happening, all I can recall is coming round afterwards and having a mark on my head and a bite mark on my tongue. I was alone at the time, but in hindsight it seems as though I might have had a seizure.

Obviously, there was a lot going on at that point, for everyone in the world – we'd all been stuck in the house for 5 months and a lot of people were suffering from depression and the added anxiety of living in a pandemic. We also had a new baby on the way. I'd been a bit sharp and snappy, which wasn't the way I'd usually be, but we had a lot going on. Maybe I was just anxious, possibly depressed? I knew something was wrong. I went to the hospital to find out what was going on, they gave me a COVID test and said it wasn't that. Kelsey and I both thought that this break would do some good for all of us.

We'd been in Norfolk a couple of days when I started feeling unwell. On the third morning, I decided I'd be better off staying in bed, so Kelsey and Aurelia went out with Kelsey's mum and aunty Julie to walk the dogs. They must have been away for about an hour. When they got back, Kelsey came up to check on me, and I vaguely remember talking to her...

The next thing I remember was waking up in the back of an ambulance. The paramedics were trying to calm me down, explaining that I'd be home within a few hours. Those hours blended into full days. Due to COVID restrictions I was alone in Norwich hospital. There were four other people on the ward and the doctor pulled the curtain around my bed to deliver the devastating news that it looked like I had a brain tumour.

I couldn't process the information, it was truly staggering. I just kept asking myself how a 32-year-old father, with a wife who was 35 weeks pregnant, could receive such world-shattering news. Lying there alone in bed, the question kept spinning around my head. I just couldn't comprehend how I'd ended up there. It was horrific. I was absolutely petrified; I couldn't stop thinking about death.

I called Kelsey immediately, still not sure of what was happening.

'I think I've got a brain tumour...'

It was an agonising ten days waiting for the results of further tests and a biopsy. It turned out to be the worst-case scenario. It was a particularly aggressive, fast-growing grade 4 brain tumour called a glioblastoma. Glioblastomas are the most common cancer that begins within the brain for adults and the world's biggest killer of all cancers for people under the age of 40. They develop spontaneously and grow rapidly, and often it takes less than three months between no brain abnormality and a fully developed tumour.

It's not known why a glioblastoma starts growing and

there isn't anything that you can do, or not do, to avoid getting one. They develop from the glial cells, which surround the nerve cells, called neurons, that we have throughout our brain and spinal cord. Glial cells support our neurons by providing them with oxygen and nutrients, as well as removing dead cells. Usually our cells grow, divide and die in a controlled way as a response to signals sent from our genes. However, sometimes mistakes can be made when the genes are copied into a new cell and these are called mutations. Mutations can cause the cells to believe that they are receiving growth signals when they aren't, or deactivate checkpoints that would usually stop cell division. When this happens, the cells continue to divide, which can develop into a tumour. The specific causes of glioblastoma development are currently still under investigation, with research examining the genetic and molecular changes in the cells.

My tumour affects the part of my brain which is responsible for movement and memory, so I struggle with walking and my short-term memory is appalling. It also affects my fine motor skills, so, for example, I can't fully open my hand up, even when I really try, which gets quite frustrating.

A prognosis is a forecast that you might be given from a doctor on what the course of your medical condition will be. When you watch a TV show and a patient gets told they have a certain amount of time to live, that is a prognosis. It comes from the doctor's experience of working with people who have similar conditions and from statistics that have been collected in the past about how other people have got on with it.

When I was first diagnosed, I would have found out the prognosis, but Kelsey and my brother Lewis stopped me. I was fishing around for a hint from the doctors, but Kelsey and Lewis thought it would be better for my mental health – especially at that time when I was in a particularly dark mental space – for me not to be given any more difficult news. I needed to be able to live with hope and they wanted to protect me from anything that would have damaged that.

When we were in Norfolk and I got that initial diagnosis, a doctor told me something very honest that has stuck with me throughout this journey.

'I can't tell you how long you've got because everybody's bodies are different,' they said. 'And I don't know how yours will react to everything.'

It's important to remember a prognosis is only some- one's best guess and for me, I'm not sure how helpful it would have been for someone to make an estimate on how long they thought I had left. I've learned the power of the mind can carry you a long way, so if someone comes and shits on your mind like that, they could really set you back. Whatever they might have said that day, I'm sure that they wouldn't have predicted I'd still be here doing half of the things I've achieved since.

Right at the start I was like a little lost puppy. I didn't really know where to wander. I didn't know what route to go down. I spent three months in bed. There was so much to contend with: I wasn't just thinking about cancer, but also how people would treat me and what they might think. I didn't want them to start treating me differently because I was living with cancer.

It was difficult to think about the future because I genuinely didn't know what it held anymore but somehow, Kelsey pulled me out of that state. She was a rock, she was just so solid through the whole process.

'Don't worry, we're going to get through this,' she'd say to me.

'How are you so strong?' I'd ask, staring at her in awe.

But she just got on with it; she kicked in and started to figure out how we were going to get through. There was a complete role switch between us that happened the moment I received my diagnosis. Now Kelsey was across everything and made a lot of the decisions for our family. I can't give her enough credit for that.

Kelsey is always focused on the solution and never the problem: she does her research by calling doctors and specialists to gather as much information as she can. With all the knowledge she has gained from the experts, she helped me to make the best decisions. It's a difficult responsibility to have and she'll forever be iconic to me for the way that she's taken it all on.

When I was first diagnosed I was using a stick and I couldn't even get out of bed. My muscles wouldn't allow it. Kelsey had to hold me up and she was 35 weeks pregnant at the time. I couldn't even walk straight. There was a time when we tried to go to Brighton and it was so cold that I seized up and couldn't move anymore.

When I'm feeling down, I can be my own worst enemy, but I always have Kelsey there to cheer me back up. She always reminds me how far I've come on this journey so far. The improvement has been incredible, but when I'm feeling low I can often overlook that.

I'd also credit Kelsey for helping me to make light of things. That's always been a big part of our relationship. We like to laugh our way through life. Laughter makes everything better, even with something like this. It brings a bit of relief to things, a bit of ease.

I think that's also been important in managing relationships with other people since my diagnosis: *How do I make people not think that I've got cancer?* I think to myself, *I'll try to be funny!*

The brain works in mysterious ways, but a healthy dose of humour has been a powerful way to diffuse tension. I even have a nurse who comes around to our house that reported back to her boss that I might be having a mental blip because of the jokes that I'd made, because it was so unusual that I was making light of my situation. Perhaps that time I'd gone a bit far. Kelsey has now banned me from making jokes around the medical staff, but the way that I look at it is, when faced with something as severe as glioblastoma, you're faced with two options: you either laugh or be sad. You pick your side and when faced with that option you have to do either one or the other – and I know which side I'm on!

Without Kelsey, I genuinely don't think I would have made it through: not only as my wife, but as a caregiver. She's been incredible. Caregivers have to be so selfless, they have to basically park all of the things that I'm sure they'd much rather be doing and devote every spare minute to those they care for. I imagine it's been tough for Kelsey to see the man that she loves go through something so challenging and I think it's been quite hard for her to swallow, that I'm not as present with the kids anymore because of everything that's happened. But we've been there for each other, got through things as best we could and discovered throughout that laughter is the way.

I've come a long way now in terms of acceptance. At times my mind has drifted to dark places, but you've got to pick yourself up and keep going, or else you'll wither away into nothingness and I don't want to do that. I've had to accept that my life has changed now, but this is still my life and I'm choosing to keep on living it.

It took me some time to become myself again, to find my way back from the Tom who spent three months in bed. It would be easy to say, 'I'm just going to lie here and die,' but I started to think maybe I was put here for a reason. And that reason is to raise more awareness about glioblastoma. Whatever happens to me, if it can have a positive effect on the treatment of glioblastoma, then that's a good thing.

'Every time we wake up in the morning is a fresh start, a new day, and that means there is always the possibility that it will be better than the last.'

15

RADIOTHERAPY & CHEMOTHERAPY

I wouldn't wish radiotherapy and chemotherapy on my worst enemy. The first treatment day I was absolutely bricking it. I caused myself a little bit of a breakdown, from having heard a lot about it, and I was anticipating it being terrible. I had watched my nan go through chemotherapy with lung cancer and I didn't know if I'd be able to deal with it myself.

Radiotherapy and chemotherapy are often presented to people with cancer diagnoses as the only options towards improvement. Sometimes there is an option to have surgery to remove the tumour, or at least part of it, but this wasn't an option for me because of where the tumour was located. The treatments for glioblastoma haven't

141

changed in the past 25 years. Often in the media we're not exposed to just how bad the side effects of treatments like radiotherapy and chemotherapy can be and how damaging they are to the person going through them.

Truly the darkest moments of this journey so far were those spent trying to pick myself up after spending a day enduring radiotherapy and chemotherapy. And I was still trying to come to terms with the fact that a doctor had told me that I was going to die soon.

I didn't really feel as though I was given any time to think about whether I wanted the treatment or not. It was assumed that this was my only choice and therefore I'd be taking it. Given that nothing else presented itself as an option, I accepted the decision, dragging myself back and forth to Guy's Hospital in Southwark, London, every day for radiotherapy treatment. It was draining as fuck. One Wednesday I was at the hospital being fitted for my mask and the day after I was starting radiotherapy.

Radiotherapy uses radiation to damage the cancer's DNA, which kills the cells. When you're starting the treatment, it takes you longer to get into position than it does to actually deliver the radiation. You lie on a table and a mask holds you in place so that you can't move. This helps the treatment to be delivered to the precise location of the tumour as accurately as possible.

To get fitted for the mask in the first place you have to go to a mould room, which is a horrendous process in itself. You breathe through a pair of straws while they put the clay over your face and shoulders so that it's a perfect fit.

The mask is important because it holds your head in place so that they can blast the tumour specifically – it would be dangerous for them to do that to your whole brain, so it has to be carefully targeted. It only takes about ten minutes, but you go in there one person and come out completely different. At times you can literally be mid-thought and feel that thought suddenly disappear due to the radiation – it's a bizarre experience. It gets easier, but the first couple of times in particular felt quite claustrophobic, being pinned in there. Coming out of it, I used to feel fried and it can make your mood change completely.

Chemotherapy uses medicines to interfere with the growth and replication of cancer cells. I would take my chemotherapy tablets about 20 minutes before I'd have radiotherapy. The idea is to try and get the chemotherapy and the radiotherapy to work together.

I was on radiotherapy for blocks of six weeks, five days a week with the weekends off, and chemotherapy constantly. Not only was it physically draining, but mentally draining as well, going up to the hospital every day for treatment. I was thankful for the mental resilience that I'd built up through experiences like auditioning for the band and touring, which allowed me to face that challenge head-on.

During all of this I was also on steroids, which I had to get on more or less as soon as I was diagnosed. These were used to protect the brain tissue and reduce swelling while I was undergoing the other two treatments. Steroids can make you aggressive and boost your testosterone, which gets your mind racing and makes it difficult to sleep. They amplify everything that you're feeling. Then you're taking drugs to try and mask the side effects of the other drugs, which means you're on even more treatments simultaneously.

When I first started going for treatment, either Kelsey or my brother Lewis would come with me, because there was always a bit of anxiety about how my body might react to the intense medication. I feel like I tolerated it pretty well. I'd try not to think too much about the treatment or the path ahead or it would become too overwhelming. And I think none of us know what is ahead in a general life sense, so I never want to think too far ahead.

Treatment days generally weren't as bad as the days that followed. The aftermath is normally when it really becomes difficult. While I was doing radiotherapy and chemotherapy, it would sort of feel okay until around week five, when suddenly it would boot me in the face.

It's impossible to put into words how it feels to go

through chemotherapy. In film and TV it's rarely depicted as much more than someone losing their hair – which is traumatic in itself – but unless you've been through it, you'll never understand how horrendous this treatment is.

I've regularly debated about whether to have the treatment or not, and of course everyone around me wants me to, but it's a more complex decision than that.

Chemotherapy leaves you with severe exhaustion and fatigue, your mind completely changes, you're so low. The chemo kills your taste buds, so you don't want to eat anymore. Your mouth is full of ulcers and your lips are covered in sores. Food becomes fuel – there is no pleasure in it anymore, everything tastes metallic. You're constantly being sick. It's like a light has been extinguished on a world that you used to know. There's too much going on and you can't cope, so you start to withdraw into yourself and lose touch with reality. You're no longer the person that you used to be. Once your course is done, you tell yourself that you never want to put yourself through that ever again.

For weeks I spent so much time on the sofa, or in bed, getting worse and worse. My fifth cycle was probably the most difficult part of this whole experience: my mind went into dark places and I couldn't face the possibility of it happening again. I decided to turn down my sixth cycle.

Despite this, I would end up returning to it later in my journey. I had to remind myself that I wanted to live.

I couldn't take that for granted. To have lived such a fulfilling life the way that I had over the past year or so, I needed to make a commitment to staying alive. I had to choose life. I didn't want to leave my kids without a dad.

At times it was easier to put a brave face on for Kelsey and the kids, but sometimes it felt good just to let it all out. While I generally have a strong and positive mindset, when you're going through times like this there are obviously severe low points as well. That's not something that I wanted to hide away from. When there are tears, we need to let them out – they're part of the healing process.

Whatever we're going through in life, when we experience an emotion we have to allow ourselves to feel it and to process it rather than avoid it. The avoidance of our feelings just leads us to feel more anxious but if we truly embrace our emotions and allow ourselves to experience them fully then there is always strength and positivity to be gained.

So many of us try to escape the way that we are feeling, or to mask our emotions as a defence mechanism, but I've learned from this journey that the best thing you can do when faced with a difficult situation is to allow yourself to feel. It's important for you to be able to cry, shout and scream. You need to really start to understand yourself, your process and how you deal with things mentally and not to bottle up your feelings. I think that men in particular can feel as though they need to stay strong and deny their true emotions, but it takes much more strength to accept what our brain is telling us. It leads to us feeling a lot clearer and experiencing life much more vividly, which I believe is key to living our best lives.

It's important to have those days where we acknowledge our negative emotions, but we can remind ourselves that every time we wake up in the morning is a fresh start, a new day, and that means there is always the possibility that it will be better than the last.

'Dave's life story is an incredible example of why all of us can have hope, no matter what challenges are placed in front of us.'

16

DAVE BOLTON

This journey has led me to find a new brother. A guy
that I talk to on a daily basis and who understands
exactly what I'm going through. A true beacon of hope,
Dave Bolton has been a huge source of inspiration to me
during this journey.

Dave's life story is an incredible example of why all of
us can have hope, no matter what challenges are placed
in front of us. He grew up with parents who were in the
military and when he turned 18, he joined the Royal Air
Force and served three years, including a four-month tour
of the Gulf as part of Air Operations Iraq. After leaving
the RAF, where he was awarded a medal for his work,
Dave began a new career with the Merseyside Police and

worked in one of the UK's most deprived areas, tackling organised crime.

When he was off duty, Dave loved riding motorbikes and one morning in 2004, he set off with a mate for a ride into Wales. His wife Samantha has since said that when she watched him set off that day, she had the feeling she might never see him again. That afternoon he was crushed by a heavy goods vehicle in an accident that could very easily have ended his life. He remained in a coma for eight days and underwent a 12-hour operation that saved him.

His leg had been scheduled for amputation and although miraculously it ended up being saved, he was told that he would never be able to walk without an aid again. This was devastating for Dave, particularly as sports and fitness played such a big part in his life. He was a keen rugby player and kickboxer, and the news meant that he would never be able to compete again.

Somehow, after 14 painful months of rehabilitation, Dave managed to return to his frontline police duties only 18 months after the accident. His hard work, determination and dedication was quite rightly celebrated with an award at the prestigious Gala Awards for policing.

Perhaps even more astonishingly, by 2009 Dave was competing in rugby union and became the Lightweight Kickboxing Champion of the World, representing Great Britain at the world championships in Italy. His ability to push past whatever expectation is put on him is truly mind-blowing, but if all of that wasn't enough trauma for one man, his biggest challenge still lay ahead.

In 2014, Dave had a seizure through the night, causing him to dislocate his shoulder and bite through his tongue. This led doctors to discover a tennis ball-sized tumour in the frontal lobe of his brain, which is typically associated with decision-making, problem-solving, thought and attention. He was able to have an operation, was given a prognosis of five years to live and deemed unfit for full duties in the police force so he took retirement due to his medical condition. He went to university to study strength and conditioning, then started his blog, Journey4Survival, to document his treatment process, as well as establishing the Ahead Of The Game foundation to support those diagnosed with cancer.

The following year, during a routine MRI brain scan, a recurrence of the tumour was discovered in the central hemisphere of Dave's brain. He ended up having his second brain surgery within 14 months and the tumour turned out to be a glioblastoma – which is the same cancer as the one I have. Dave was given a prognosis of three months without treatment, or six to eight months with radiotherapy and chemotherapy. He opted for the treatment, but in the last week of a six-week course, he suffered a psychotic breakdown and was admitted to hospital.

Incredibly, Dave has fought his way through all of this and it's been seven years now since he was given that prognosis. He's one of the lucky ones and he's the proof I really needed to see that with hope and determination, you can live a fairly normal life with glioblastoma.

Dave has used his story to inspire so many others, from businesses and charities to sports teams and others who are living with cancer, so he was quickly notified of my story when we shared it with the press, thanks to a flood of notifications from people on social media. He's the type of guy who just wants to use his powers for good, in any way that he can, so he reached out to me immediately. Unfortunately, I didn't see it – or at least I didn't at first.

Coincidentally, Kelsey later came across him online and sent him a message on Instagram. I believe that Dave Bolton was destined to come into my life and I'm a much stronger person as a result, thanks to the relationship that I've built with him.

When people say 'I can imagine what you're going through', while I appreciate it as a nice sentiment, the truth is that the vast majority can't imagine what I'm going through at all. Dave is the rare person for me that can honestly say he's been through the exact same experience, faced the same situation and had the same thoughts. It's incredibly bonding to feel so alone in what you're dealing with and then find someone else who understands.

We quickly became very close. During the first six months after I was diagnosed I would call Dave daily, asking for advice: 'Is this right?', 'I feel like this – what's going on?' He's been there for me during some of the darkest moments.

I remember one night I was having these searing headaches that were scaring the shit out of me. I hadn't experienced anything like it and I was sure that this couldn't be good. I called Dave.

'I'm really scared.'

'What's up?' he asked.

'I've got these headaches …'

'Those headaches are natural, mate. I had the same feeling as well,' explained Dave, calmly.

I could immediately feel the anxiety starting to dissolve inside of me.

Knowing that Dave had been through this too, and knew exactly what the treatments were, was the reassurance I needed. And to be honest, that reassurance could only really have come from someone like him. Even the doctors I was in contact with hadn't actually felt what this was like. When you're dealing with something as brutal as glioblastoma and you've reached the point where I'm at, there's not many people you can turn to. Statistically, only 25 per cent of people will make it past a year with what we've got. When you factor in that Dave was the same age as me when he was diagnosed and also has a young family, you begin to see just how extraordinary it was that I would come to find such a relatable figure to find inspiration from.

Dave said that he'd had a similar experience with a girl he'd found in America called Cheryl Broyles. Cheryl had been living with glioblastoma for eight years and he reached out to her via email and that helped spark that hope in him that there was the possibility of living a normal life despite such poorly stacked odds. He provided that feeling for us.

When Kelsey was spending hours a day researching treatments and building her knowledge of what might be able to help us through, Dave was able to guide her on the information that is accurate and relevant. As I'm sure you can imagine, there are plenty of very negative rabbit holes you can find yourself down when looking up this stuff, particularly on the internet, and that can be completely destructive to having a positive mindset. You're advised not to look things up online, but of course in our society and how reliant we've become on it, curiosity can get the better of you. With Dave's help we were able to keep things fairly filtered and stay focused on what would be productive in the healing process.

I have confidence and trust in Dave. We call each other brothers, even though we've only actually met in person four times. Sometimes it can be quite tricky when everyone around you has their opinion on what's best for you and while I totally appreciate that it's all rooted in love, it can make decision-making tough. Dave is someone that I can sound off all of these thoughts to, to help me make sense of what I think is best for me. During the process of writing this book I was faced with a difficult decision about whether or not to put myself through another round of chemotherapy. After talking to him, I decided despite how tough it is, it would be worth it.

Dave and I are rare. Understandably, when you're sitting in that doctor's room, facing someone who has gone through years of medical training and experience telling you that you have a cancer that is likely to kill you within three months, a lot of people accept that. It's all too easy to lose all hope. That's why it's been important to Dave to share his story and now for me to share mine too. I can't tell you how much of a difference inspiration makes to get you through any obstacle that you're faced with in life. Hearing stories that go against the statistics is incredibly motivational. It's proof that you don't have to just accept what is handed to you. You can take matters into your own hands and live life the way you want to live it.

It's been vital to me to know that Dave is out there living a fulfilling life. He was, and continues to be, an invaluable source of information and hope. And I think it shouldn't go unsaid that this isn't something he's only doing for me. Dave works solely on the rehabilitation of people with cancer now and I imagine that's really difficult work to do. He's lost people that he's become close to, which has been very painful for him, but he understands his role in the greater good. He tells me that the positives he gets from helping others far outweigh the negative parts and I have nothing but respect for how deeply he cares for them.

'I think that optimism is vital in getting you through any challenge in life.'

17

FURTHER TREATMENTS

I was offered radiotherapy and chemotherapy by the NHS, but that was that. I'm a very inquisitive person by nature, so, not content with the options that I'd been presented with, I have accessed further treatments including new experimental drugs and holistic therapies which have each played an important part in my journey. Kelsey and I started researching other options out there and began reaching out to specialists from all around the world. Soon the joke in our house became: 'Which country are we calling tonight?'

Most of the treatments that can be used for glioblastoma are still in trial stages and can currently only be accessed privately. Drug trials take years and cost a fortune to deliver, but when you're living with cancer, you just want to know that you have the opportunity to have the latest science on your side so that you are able to live on the best way you can.

It's a very difficult disease to treat so I've been open-minded about what we would try. The reality of glioblastoma, because it's such a fast-moving disease, is that death is always a possibility. It's a disease that doesn't go away, but the aim is to keep it as stable as possible and not let it get too crazy. I don't want to just chuck anything and everything at it, but I do want to make sure that I'm taking things that are going to have a strong shot at fighting the tumour and don't have too much of a negative impact on my body.

Not that many people are able to access private treatments and I think that needs to change. Right now, the harsh reality is that how much treatment you're able to access is dependent on how wealthy you are. I'm fortunate that my success with The Wanted, and some help from friends along the way, has meant that I've been able to afford a lot of the treatments that many wouldn't.

I'd always approach a new treatment with confidence – I think it's really important to put your belief into each new approach, otherwise you're not going to get the full benefit of what they can offer. I think that optimism is vital in getting you through any challenge in life and that is even more the case when you're facing cancer. Speaking to others who have inspirational stories and positive experiences really helps with that. I talk to people in hospital waiting rooms who had been through treatments themselves and that really helps me to have a positive mindset.

I made friends with people who were on the same treatment days as me. I'd call them my 'cancer friends' and we'd keep each other company and support each other in the waiting rooms. It was good to have others to share my experiences with who had been through the same as me, and it was reassuring to hear about their experiences.

There are so many different treatments out there that it starts to get quite complicated. The doctors would introduce you to something new and I'd be like, 'But what is that? What does it actually do? Does it cure cancer?' It's heavy. The travelling backwards and forwards for the treatments is tiring enough, never mind trying to get your head around what everything means.

There is also an ethical dilemma in giving these treatments to people in similar situations to me, who will experience more harm than good from them. They can compromise quality of life in favour of prioritising quantity of time – which can mean living in hell for months in order to extend life by potentially just a few weeks. The decision as to whether or not to take on each new treatment needs careful consideration. It's all a learning curve: learning about your own body, what it can take and what it can do.

One of the reasons for sharing my story and spreading awareness is the hope that more treatments will become available through the NHS in the future. Kelsey and I decided to set out on trying a range of experimental treatments. Some of them are very expensive and because you are on several treatments at the same time, it's impossible to know which are working and which aren't. But when my back is against the wall I feel like I must exhaust every option. That's the risk that I choose to take in the fight for my life.

When initially looking for an oncologist it all came down to reputation: who has saved the most people? However, I found through working with multiple doctors that it is equally important to find someone who is able to work in a way that fits your own philosophy and mindset. I've had doctors who have frowned at my use of cannabis when it was the only thing giving me any proper pain relief, as if it's any worse than the heavy-duty drugs that they were prescribing me. It's very frustrating when you find a treatment that you want to try and your oncologist is closed-off to it – a drug is only as good as the doctor is with that drug.

My current oncologist Omar and his nurse Vicky are phenomenal, they're very understanding and supportive and have very quickly become a big part of our lives. They've done so much to make sure we get the information that we need as soon as possible. They are more experimental and open to different ideas than the other oncologists I've come across and that fits with my approach.

For Kelsey and me, it felt natural to explore alternative therapy. Our mums are both a little bit outside the box and my mum is really into crystals and stuff, so it's always been a part of our lives.

I've been doing daily meditation since I received my diagnosis. I'll admit that I wasn't a huge fan of it prior to this cancer journey, but it really helps me to calm myself and focus on the present. I'm now up to doing half an hour, which has been hard work because at first, I found it very difficult to focus. But practice makes perfect. Now I can sit there and close myself off from everything, switch off from life. I follow a guided meditation on YouTube and it's been incredibly helpful when my mind starts to get a bit too hectic. I'd honestly recommend it to anyone who needs a bit of a break from a busy day. I know it can seem a little bit daunting at first, but looking at where I was when I started practising meditation to where I'm at now, I think if I can do it then anyone can!

There's a whole world out there and we're often guilty of just taking what has been accepted in the West. I think that during that first four or five months after my diagnosis I don't think there was a doctor or practitioner in the world that I didn't get in touch with. I've worked with cranial osteopaths, energy healers, Ayurvedic practitioners and homeopaths to name just a few.

I think that sometimes the holistic stuff isn't embraced by Western doctors, but in my personal experience a lot of it actually supports their treatments and practices anyway. The important thing is to find the combination of things that feels like it's making a difference to you, treatments that you believe in. I've been undergoing holistic treatments that boost my immune system and NHS drugs that maintain my stability and stop me from getting worse.

I think one of the key things that you get from engaging with holistic treatments is the feeling of having some autonomy back, that you have a say in what's happening to your body and that you're being proactive about healing. After going through radiotherapy and chemotherapy, where it felt like I had no control over what's happening to me, that was an incredibly positive and refreshing experience.

There's not many people who are diagnosed with glioblastoma who get a year down the line and get their tumour to a stable state like I did. Despite all of the trouble that it caused earlier in my life, I honestly do credit cannabis for that. While it can't currently be prescribed legally in the UK, almost all of the doctors I've spoken to on this journey mentioned that it could help. I started to take a few drops of cannabis oil every evening very shortly after my diagnosis. At the very least I can say it definitely stimulated my appetite and that's a good thing for someone who's going through cancer treatment. Perhaps even more importantly, it's made me laugh at things. The cannabis oil helps you to bring out a side of yourself that wouldn't be accessible to you during a course of chemotherapy. The laughs we had on our Wanted WhatsApp group with our manager Damo every night after I'd had my cannabis oil were hilarious and truly special. I hope that chat never gets out, it would get me in a lot of trouble.

Exploring other treatments, whether or not they've been clinically proven, has stimulated positive thinking in me and the power of the mind is so important. I think whatever you choose to go with, you have to believe that it is going to work for you; your mindset has to be powerful.

Getting to where I am now has taken a lot of patience, which I think has been a key lesson for me as I've gotten older. You've got to have patience with people and situations. I'm a very reactive person, so when I was younger if something happened that annoyed me, I'd go steaming in without even thinking first. Now, I've learned to digest information a little bit better before making a decision or responding to something, which has been integral to finding the treatments that work for me; a little patience can really go a long way in terms of gaining perspective and being more understanding of the scenarios you find yourself in, and the people that you deal with, on a daily basis.

I like to track my progress by looking back over my brain scans and seeing how things have changed. It gives me a focus. It lets me know what I've got to work towards. When I got the news in January 2021 that there had been a significant reduction in the tumour, I was ecstatic. I knew that we were doing something right and just had to continue on. That always gave me the hope I needed to keep on living my life.

I think a lot of this journey is about how I feel. Every time I sit down with a doctor the first thing they ask me is, 'How do you feel?' That's quite a big part of it. If I felt like shit, then there was a problem: 'Why do you feel like shit?' Then we have to do some further investigation. That is something that I think we should all be aware of, regardless of what we're going through. If we feel a certain way, either physically or emotionally, then that is our body telling us that there is something we need to investigate. If we wake up and we're feeling down, we have the power to figure out the root of it. That self-awareness will help us to make sense of our feelings and move towards a more positive mindset.

'Having kids
has taught me
that you can
get through
anything.'

18

BODHI

Our son, Bodhi Thomas Paris Parker, was born on 20 October 2020, not too long after I'd been given my diagnosis. It was a very difficult time, trying to work around my treatment but also the COVID-19 pandemic, which added further complication and protocol to the process.

One night we were watching *The Only Way Is Essex* in bed and all you could see was Kelsey's belly going mental.

'You're not going into labour, are you?' I asked.

'No, don't be ridiculous,' she snapped back at me. 'We've still got two weeks to go until the due date!'

At the end of the episode she stood up and her waters broke.

I was like, 'Are you pissing yourself?'

We'd been hoping for a home birth, especially under the circumstances, but Bodhi wasn't ready. The next morning, I had to go for my radiotherapy treatment and when I got home Kelsey had spent her entire day bouncing on a birthing ball, trying to persuade Bodhi that it was time to come out and join us.

In the end we had to call the hospital at 3am because she still hadn't gone into labour. I went with her and the staff at the hospital were really accommodating: they went above and beyond what they had to do for us and kept us contained to one room because of my vulnerable position. We were so lucky to have them because a lot of hospitals weren't allowing partners on to the labour wards because of COVID restrictions.

It was a very intense time and I wasn't really all there because of my treatment. After Bodhi was born, Kelsey sent me home so that I could get some rest before travelling back into central London the next morning. I was only able to have one day off radiotherapy. It was incredibly difficult to leave my wife and newborn son in the hospital and drag myself away to treatment the next day, but it was the best thing for all of us in the bigger picture.

We had the name Bodhi in mind for a few years, and always planned to use it if we had a son. It means enlightenment and awakening, which feels fitting given the time of his arrival into our lives; a time where we have learned so much and adapted to understanding life in a completely new way.

The obsession I'd had with Aurelia when she was born made my limited involvement with Bodhi – because of my treatment – all the more difficult to accept. At least because I knew how well things turned out for Aurelia, I had confidence that Bo would be alright.

Bodhi is a bit of a mummy's boy. He cries a lot, but as soon as Kelsey picks him up he stops crying straight away. I'm like, 'Wow!'

Bodhi wanders around the house looking for me, and when I see him he fills me with a sense of purpose. Despite everything that is going on with me, having another baby brings more light into every day. Having kids has taught me that you can get through anything. Even with the difficult conditions around Bodhi's birth, I believe we were meant to have a baby at that time. As Kelsey always says, 'Is it ideal for your husband to be diagnosed with a brain tumour when you're 35 weeks pregnant in the middle of a global pandemic? Probably not.' But what's meant to be is meant to be.

Life doesn't throw anything at us that we can't deal with, even if at times the obstacles we're facing might seem impossible. There is always something there to be learned and some hope in the future, so we just have to normalise the circumstances that are in front of us and deal with them the best way that we can. If you put your mind to it, you can get through anything. That's something I would like Aurelia and Bodhi to understand about their mum and dad in the future and apply to their own lives. Bringing kids into this world is a challenge, for everybody, but overcoming that is testament to our power and resilience as humans and how magical the gift of life really is.

Being a father really changes your outlook on life. When I was younger, I'd love being out on tour with the band, or staying out in the clubs with Kelsey until the early hours, but now I can't wait to get home. I just love being with the kids and tucking them into bed before they go to sleep. I find it really tough spending time away from them. Fatherhood makes you grow up very quickly. It's very easy to overthink being a parent, but we just do the best we can, which I think is the only way that you can approach parenting.

I want my kids to have financial security to live their lives the way they want to. I don't want them ever to have to worry about money, or make decisions based on covering their basic needs. I hope that I've set up a life for them where they are free to pursue their own purpose, unhindered. Aurelia is an outgoing, go-getter kind of girl and she will just drag me along. And Bodhi is a very patient boy – he's taught me massive things actually, like how patience is huge. Teaching the kids how to walk and talk and eat by themselves, you have to take your time.

I get to see the kids every morning before we have to go and get on with our days. We're all becoming increasingly busy – I often have to go and get treatment and Aurelia has just started nursery – but we always make that time first thing. Just sitting there watching TV and cuddling the kids empowers me for whatever is to come and sets me up for the day. You don't realise until you have your own kids what love really is. I'd happily give my life up for them, that's what they mean to me.

Family is the most important thing that we have on this earth and yet we can all take that for granted at times. Of course there will be fights and disagreements, but that unconditional love you have for those closest to you is to be cherished and never overlooked. I'm really proud of everything that I've achieved in my career. I'm thankful for all of the success that's brought with it and the once-in-a-lifetime opportunities afforded me but nothing will ever come close to how I feel about the family that Kelsey and I have built together. I think it's really important that we never lose sight of how much our loved ones contribute to our lives and to make sure that they know that they're appreciated.

'I wanted to create something that would inspire people.'

19

STAND UP TO CANCER

After regaining hope and finding therapies that actually seemed to be doing me some good, I needed to get my strength back. If I was going to keep living life on my own terms, I knew I wouldn't be doing it as a patient going through radiotherapy every week.

Everyone living with cancer has the right to make an individual decision about how much detail, if any, they wish to share about their cancer journey and I have a great respect for whatever anyone chooses. It was important for me to be as transparent as possible about mine, because I believed it could be powerful in helping other people. It wasn't an easy decision to let cameras into my house to make a documentary, do interviews on daytime television, or to write this book, but I felt driven to spread awareness of brain tumours, which can hopefully help make a difference. I hope that part of my legacy will be to contribute to a change in how brain cancer research is funded.

When I learned that only 1 per cent of the cancer research budget in the UK goes to exploring brain tumour treatment, it was a wake-up moment for me. I wanted to find a way to use my platform to advocate for others like myself who were living with this disease. My aim was to raise awareness of brain tumours to the general public. I knew that with my profile as a pop star, if I made a film about glioblastomas, it would reach a wider audience than a less personal documentary on the subject. I wanted to create something that would inspire people, rather than dwell solely on the sadness of the situation so I came up with a goal for myself: I wanted to perform at the Royal Albert Hall to raise money for Stand Up to Cancer and the National Brain Appeal, and I wanted that process to be documented. I teamed up with Channel 4 and the amazing Nick Bullen at Spun Gold, who I'd worked with on *The Real Full Monty*, to create the *Inside My Head* documentary, which aired in October 2021, a year after my diagnosis. I'm touched to say that it has since been watched by millions of people.

Stepping back into the spotlight wasn't easy. The person that I was in the band was so different to the one that

I am now, but I knew this was my purpose. I wanted to be up there performing, which would be a huge challenge, but I thought it would make all the difference in spreading awareness of this disease and raising funding for vital research.

While fame gave me a voice and a platform that I could use for good, sharing my story definitely left me feeling massively exposed and vulnerable at times. There was a lot of pressure for me to be this inspirational figure, and to stay positive, which is why I think that showing the reality of living with cancer – in a very honest way – was important to me. I wanted to really show how powerful a sense of hope can be in allowing you to live fully and happily, against even the most adverse situations.

Naturally, some days are more difficult than others and at times I really struggled with having to show up to a TV studio to talk, or to have a production team filming me for the day, but I remained focused on the bigger picture. It's important to be transparent, to show that while I do maintain a positive mindset for the majority of the time, the reality is that I'm facing a very difficult set of circumstances every day. I think that the truth is really what makes this experience all the more enlightening. Crying, being in bed, not wanting to get up is a necessary part of the process and it's getting through those lows that make me feel so positive when I'm having a good day.

From the outset, I intended for the show to be fun and joyous. I wanted people to leave saying it was the best show they had ever been to; I didn't want it to be sad. It also provided me with a bit of light at the end of the tunnel. I love performing, it's where I feel most at home, so to be able to get back out there and to sing in front of people gave me something to work towards. You sink or swim in situations like this and this show was the motivation I needed to flick that switch and pull myself together.

I sat down with my manager, Damien Sanders, to come up with a wish list of artists that I wanted to come and play at the show. Pretty much from the moment I was diagnosed, Ed Sheeran reached out to me with an offer to do anything he could to help, so it made sense for him to be top of my list. I've never publicly said this before (and he'll probably be mad that I'm doing it now) but Ed is a very special man, he even helped out with my medical bills when I was seeking other treatment options and having private immunotherapy treatment. He didn't need to do any of that, but Kelsey and I were so grateful to him for his support, it meant the world.

Another person who helped me financially was my old boss, Ashley Tabor – I say boss as he was *the* guy and biggest brain behind The Wanted. Again, he will hate me saying this but tough – some things need to be said. Saying thank you just doesn't seem enough for what Ed and Ash did, but at least I can thank them publicly.

Next, we got Sigrid, Becky Hill and KSI, and then we gave Harry from McFly a call. McFly put on a banging show – I'd seen them live a couple of times and they always bring the house down. I felt like they would be a great addition to the line-up I was putting together.

In the back of my mind what I really hoped for was that we could get the rest of the boys to join me for a reunion. It would be the first time The Wanted had appeared live in seven years. I reached out to each of them individually to see whether they'd be up for it and everyone seemed positive about it. That was exciting, but I knew that we'd only really know if it was going to be possible if we got together to see what our chemistry was like after such a long time. Since it was still the middle of the pandemic and there were a lot of restrictions in place, we organised a Zoom call to catch up. It says something about our time as a band that after all of those years apart, from the second their faces flashed up on that screen, I felt completely at ease. Of course we'd had our friction and falling-outs in the past, but that happens with all families and we'd been through too much together to hold on to any negativity. It was all smiles, jokes and excitement. It felt like the old days again and completely natural that we were discussing our next performance together.

Even when years go by and we haven't been in touch, speaking to the boys always feels like no time has passed at all, it's like nothing has ever changed. We have a bond that I don't think could ever be broken, no matter what happens.

We'd never played the Royal Albert Hall before, which I think is part of the reason I wanted to host the show there. It's such a sensational venue, a truly epic place, and I knew that it would be the right setting to have a night to remember. Once I went there to have a look at it I couldn't wait for the night of the show – but at the same time I was shitting myself about it! At that point there was no going back, we were doing this show and it was going to make a difference.

It's a bit strange asking people to do stuff for you, but I knew it was important to put together an incredible line-up and it was time to ask for some help. Despite the past behind One Direction and The Wanted, I was so happy to see Liam Payne reach out to me on Instagram immediately, asking if there was anything he could do to help. When Liam heard about my story he was really touched by it and told me that he had been inspired by my strength and courage, so I asked him to join me to be a part of the Stand Up to Cancer show and he agreed without hesitation. I really appreciated that from him, particularly given the history between us and One Direction. I think that when we connected on a Zoom call to talk about the gig, it was the first time we'd actually spoken to one another so I was a little bit anxious about how it might go, but he was lovely and couldn't have been more helpful. He's a really

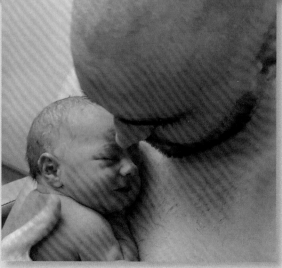

My first time meeting Aurelia and Bodhi. I wouldn't have missed either of your births for the world.

Nap time – Aurelia left, Bodhi below. The best things that ever happened to me.

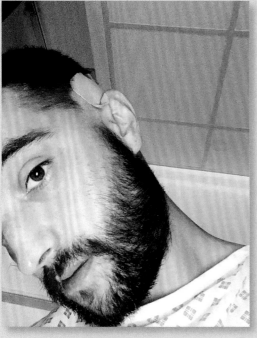

Getting through one day at a time, with the best friends around me.

© Anthony Devlin/Stringer/Getty Images

Right and below: HITS Live in Birmingham, November 2021, with the lads.

© Anthony Devlin/Stringer/Getty Images

On the Most Wanted tour, together.

Family...

Means...

Everything.

good guy. It meant the world to me that he was reaching out and offering to perform. I knew the fans would really appreciate it too.

When you put things into perspective, it makes you think we were pathetic kids arguing over nothing back then. Now, years down the line, you look at things in a totally different way. I look at Liam and think, what a great person to accept what had happened in the past and to offer to collaborate with me on this show anyway. Life has changed a lot since we had a falling-out with One Direction. We've both grown up and had kids of our own. I think our priorities are with them now more than ourselves.

We'd set the date for the show when I started chemotherapy. At the time it was nine months away and that gave me a vital focal point, something to work towards that I was determined to achieve. Following the process of radiotherapy and chemotherapy, and how weak that leaves the body, I needed to find ways to build my strength so that I'd be able to stand there on that stage and sing. I couldn't let everyone down, so I knew I had to repair my body so that it was strong enough to be able to perform. Not only did that require me to have physio, but I needed vocal coaching as the chemo had affected my speech.

One of my big fears around that time was that my voice might not be there when it came to do the performance. It had been deteriorating through the course of my treatment and I knew that it would take some intense vocal coaching to bring it back. I started to have Steven Luke Walker come to the house to help me train and I would be very careful not to use the extent of my range. I was terrified that if I attempted a note that was too high, my voice might crack and end up lost for good. We ended up booking a private rehearsal room one day so that I could be alone with Steven and test how far I could push myself. I knew that if I was going to be singing at the Royal Albert Hall and that was going to be televised, I had to give it my best shot. I remember that sense of relief washing over me when I first let go of those reservations and went for it: my voice was still there!

I felt like I needed to get my arm and leg working properly, so that I would be able to move around the stage for the show. I felt quite embarrassed and vulnerable about the fact that I was unable move as I previously could and I didn't want the audience to notice so I started to really focus on my physio.

As the performance was drawing closer, I was conscious of the fact that my movement was beginning to deteriorate again. I was so determined to make it to the show, but naturally there was doubt creeping into my mind from time to time, that little voice on my shoulder questioning whether all of this would be possible. Luckily, I'd developed quite a lot of mental resilience by this point in the process and I was able to keep my thoughts positive and get support from the boys to help make things work.

By the time it came to the show, I was more anxious about my movement than my singing. There were a lot of people who had paid money for tickets and I wanted them to be impressed, I didn't want to give them a below-par performance.

In rehearsals the boys worked with me to adapt our set so that I was always supported on stage. We looked for ways to choreograph the performance around my limited range of movement. Max literally held me up at one point! It was really lovely to have us all back together, working for the same thing – to put on a great show and for a cause that was so close to my heart. I'll always have great memories of that night and I'm so glad that I made the decision to do it in the first place. It was such an amazing feeling to be with The Wanted on stage again and for such a beautiful purpose.

I wasn't prepared for the overwhelming emotion that poured through me at the end of that show. Despite the mammoth task I'd set for myself, against almost impossible odds, I'd made it onto the stage that night and given it my all. If that's not proof that we can overcome any challenge we're faced with, then I don't know what is.

'I want others to feel empowered, whether they have cancer or not, to know that they can always reclaim the path that their life is taking.'

20

ACTIVISM

I think that one of the most important things that I can achieve with writing this book is to spread awareness about brain tumours and in particular the low amount of funding that goes into research around them. Glioblastomas are one of the world's deadliest cancers. They're the biggest killer of any cancer in people under 40 and yet brain tumours only receive 1 per cent of all the funding that goes into cancer research. An increase in funding for brain cancer research can help things progress and improve in the near future. Glioblastomas are currently considered incurable, but with more research, I believe that this could change.

When you look at the phenomenal success of breast

cancer research and the work that's being done there, the survival rates are really high, but they have over the years received a much larger percentage of the funding. I'm by no means suggesting that they should have any less, but it is proof that with more funding progress can be made. If the current level of funding that's being invested into brain cancer continues, it's been estimated that it will take another 100 years to get anywhere close to where breast cancer research is right now.

Activism around this has become very important to me. I want to be part of the change towards more investment in brain cancer research, so that there is a lot more hope for people who are diagnosed in the future.

As I've said earlier, a lot of the drugs out there are still considered experimental and are stuck at the stage where they're not approved for widespread use. We're lucky to have the NHS, but when fighting a disease like glioblastoma and certain treatments aren't available because of their experimental status, you have to go private and pay for them – and that's if you're lucky enough to be able to afford it, which doesn't sit right with me at all. Everybody should have the same chance at being able to fight disease. It shouldn't be the case that you need money to be able to afford the best chance of staying alive.

Because brain cancers are still considered relatively rare, it's very difficult to get the structure in place to be able to develop new drugs. That requires funding to cover training, trials, research – so many different things. The UK is one of the worst-performing countries for outcomes in brain cancer. It's ridiculous that so little has advanced with brain cancer research and that's all due to a lack of funding because there's not enough awareness about it.

I started to feel as though it was a moral obligation to educate others about brain cancer, so that maybe I could make some kind of impact that would help people who are diagnosed in the future. It also felt like a way of honouring those who have been through it and have passed away, so that all of us aren't going through this in vain. I feel a connection to anyone who has shared, or will share, this experience, past, present and future. As Dave Bolton always puts it, 'I'm in a club that nobody wants to be part of!'

A cure will never happen in my lifetime, but because of my pop career I have a platform that will allow me to share this information with people who might otherwise not know about it. I wanted to use my voice to make a positive impact for all of us in the club, so that at least over time things can get better.

During the filming of *Inside My Head* I had the opportunity to go to the House of Commons. I called Dave Bolton the night before and he came along with me and Maria Lester to talk to 50 MPs and Lords.

Maria Lester's brother Stephen died at the age of 26 from a brain tumour in 2011 and she petitioned for more government funding as a result. If you manage to get more than 100,000 people to sign a petition, then it has to be spoken about in the House of Commons and Maria managed to get 250,000 signatures. It was agreed that more funding would be allocated to brain tumour research and they promised to contribute £60 million across five years and by that point – which was ten years later – they had still only given £6 million. We were told that it's difficult for them to secure the money as there hasn't been any new research, but how can there be any further developments without funding? This is the paradox that we're facing in our work to move things forward but while we have a voice, we need to keep going and pushing for progress that will benefit future generations.

We asked them why people end up having to set up their own GoFundMe pages to go to countries like France, Israel and Canada that offer better treatments than we have over here in the UK. They think we're world leaders, but in our opinion we were actually one of the worst – still focusing everything on chemotherapy derived from the 1950s instead of looking further afield and taking inspiration from what else is out there.

I asked them about their thoughts on cannabis, which might have been a bit cheeky, and they kindly told me that – while it was a good question – this probably wasn't the place to discuss it! I explained that it's not for recreational use, I'm not taking it because I want to – and Dave used to be in the drug squad! But it's necessary to get through the pain, particularly early on. It's THC stripped from the cannabis bud, super concentrated, thick oil – like tar. When you take a drop at first you basically just pass out, then you have to build your tolerance daily as you go, taking a tiny bit every evening just to keep going.

I was really proud to be there with Dave and Maria, saying our bit about brain cancer in the House of Commons. It's an opportunity to persuade those who have power to make changes because that's the only way it's going to happen really. We were invited to join the All-Party Parliamentary Group on Brain Tumours (APPGBT), which was established in 2005 to raise political awareness on the issues facing those in the brain tumour community, from those living with brain cancer to their families, researchers and clinicians.

I think that what we've all just been through with COVID proves that there is always a way to fight disease if it's given enough attention and research. The COVID vaccine was developed so quickly and yet for decades no progress has been made with brain tumours, let alone finding a cure. Let's get the greatest brains together and figure out a solution.

Cancer doesn't only take its toll on you: it's not just your cancer, it's your family's cancer, your friends' cancer, everybody around you is affected by it. I think people forget about caregivers and the impact that it has on them. Obviously, this has been tough for me, but it's also been incredibly difficult for Kelsey and she's managed to pull me through the darkest times with her seemingly impenetrable ability to find positivity and light in every situation. It's also been amazing connecting with people living with cancer around the world and finding strength in the stories that they share. I've come into contact with so many different people since my diagnosis and learned that no two cancer journeys are the same. There is an incredibly diverse community, all living their lives with various forms of cancer, and every single one of them is incredibly inspiring. As someone who is living with cancer myself, I feel like it's my duty to give back to that community by doing anything I can to help others through their journey or at least make it a little more palatable by sharing my story. I'm proud of where I've got to, having already exceeded the expectations of my initial diagnosis and managing to find stability in both my cancer but also my life as well. I want others to feel empowered, whether they have cancer or not, to know that they can always reclaim the path that their life is taking and to live it the way that they want to.

'I could hear the chants: "We want Tom!"'

21

HOME AGAIN

While you're going through the rehabilitation necessary to bring you back from cancer treatments, you might not be surprised to hear that you spend quite a lot of time sitting around the house in front of the TV. That means that you watch a lot of daytime shows and for me that particularly meant lots of game shows. You can't imagine how excited I was to hear that my bandmate Max and I had been invited to appear on an episode of *Pointless Celebrities*.

I was buzzing to be there with Max in front of hosts Alexander Armstrong and Richard Osman. It was surreal to be actually playing in the studio after I'd spent so many afternoons shouting my answers at the television in my living room. I got us off to a good start and I was genuinely surprised when we started doing really well. We managed to get to the final and rather than choose to answer questions about 'Actors Who Have Played Musketeers', Max quite rightly suggested we go for 'Sporting Defeats'.

We were playing to win money for Brain Tumour Research and the Brain Cancer Charity, so I really wanted to get a pointless answer – which in case you haven't seen the show (where have you been?!) means a correct answer to the question that nobody came up with when the producers of the show asked 100 people.

Max said he had three answers for the category 'Mens teams that lost a FIFA World Cup match by four goals or more'. He knows his football, so I put my trust in him, but I'd be lying if I said I wasn't nervous. His first response was Panama. It was a correct answer. We watched as the counter ran down from 100; it was getting closer and closer to the bottom. I couldn't believe that Max had done it on the first go – let's be honest, he hadn't been great in the earlier rounds! It stopped at one. One person in their survey had answered Panama!

'I hate that person!' I joked.

We were down to two answers.

Max's second response, Algeria, went up on the board. That one had been a guess, he said. It sat there for a second, then was replaced by a big red X. It was incorrect – the win was slipping away from us.

Saudi Arabia was his third answer. He was more confident in this one but it was definitely nerve-wracking to think that this was our last chance to win the money that would go to a cause that was obviously so important to me. I could feel the butterflies fluttering around my stomach, my heart banging in my chest. The countdown appeared on the screen: it was another correct answer. But had any of the people surveyed by *Pointless Celebrities* also got it? The number started to run down, from 100. It passed the halfway mark and then started slowing down as it came towards the lower numbers. I watched it pass ten, then five. It was decelerating, creeping down digit by digit, until … zero! It was a *Pointless* answer!

I was over the moon. It was already surreal to be in the studio, but to have won the jackpot and for that to help me on my broader mission to spread awareness about Brain Cancer, what an afternoon! I was so pleased to have had Max playing along with me, he absolutely smashed it in getting us that win.

And now every afternoon when I tune in to watch Alexander and Richard, and to play along from my sofa, I can look smugly at that coveted *Pointless* trophy perched on my mantelpiece.

When you get told that you're potentially going to die within 18 months, it's pretty hard-hitting to say the least. But to be honest with you, the best thing to do is to put it to the back of your mind and just crack on.

I've realised that since my diagnosis, a lot of people want to ask how I'm getting on. I think people are a lot more in tune with how I'm feeling, which is really lovely. I do appreciate that, it's really nice of them, but it's also bittersweet because it shouldn't take a life-threatening diagnosis for us to ask each other how we're doing. I think that's a world problem: we're all guilty of living the fast life and not checking in with each other. That's something I'd really like to come out of this situation, for people to ask each other how they're doing – it shouldn't need a cancer diagnosis for people to check on each other and how they are feeling.

Right now, I'm trying to ignore the cancer as much as possible and just get on with my life. I have a family and an increasingly busy job to do, so it's really important that I'm able to normalise my situation as much as possible. Since the show at the Royal Albert Hall, The Wanted have released *Most Wanted: Greatest Hits* and we're getting ready to go on tour. I've also continued to build on my passion for dance music and I launched a new project called Lost + Found with my mate Ollie Marland, which I'm looking forward to continuing to build on.

As I write this, I'm preparing myself physically and

mentally to go on a 12-date arena tour with The Wanted. It's going to be fun, but intense to say the least. I'm building up towards it by doing physio and there is a lot more logistical planning to do than usual, which is saying something! We're going to have a dedicated medication person on tour, because otherwise I'll forget. And I'll be facing the biggest crowds that I have played to in years. I'm excited for it, but I'd be lying if I said there weren't some nerves as well. I'm sure after the first day of rehearsals I'll be absolutely bollocked.

After a few weeks of treatment at a wellness clinic in Spain, and how gutted I was about missing the first couple of shows, I was overcome with emotion as I was helped onto the riser by the rest of the boys. They had already played through most of the hits.

Every night, Martin would say the same thing that he's said for 13 years: 'Boys, let's go do a show!'

That instinct was in me to want to get up and perform, but I knew I had to hang on for the first hour. I felt ready to get up there. It's where I was born to be. That's what I've been doing my whole life. But I had to be reasonable in what I could manage. Even appearing for this encore was pushing myself further than anyone had expected me to be able to achieve.

I just wanted to be able to experience that feeling again, of being in front of those who had grown with us on our journey as The Wanted. Our fans had always been there for us every step of the way – buying the CDs, tickets, T-shirts, posting about us online. This story wouldn't be half of what it is without those people and I wanted to be with them, even if it was just for a few minutes.

A countdown was running on the massive screen above our heads. I could hear the chants: 'We want Tom!' We prepared to be elevated in front of the packed-out arena, who were all in anticipation of seeing me.

When the timer hit one, we were pushed up onto the stage, 'Gold Forever' blaring out of the speakers, the boys by my side. The ocean of fans, their phone lights twinkling for as far as I could see. The first verse is a duet. It's me and Max:

Say my name like it's the last time,
Live today like it's your last night,
We want to cry but we know it's alright,
Cause I'm with you and you're with me.

No matter what happens to me, that rush I get when I'm on stage will never go away. For everything that I've been through in my life, I don't think that will ever change. I was born and raised in Tonge Moor, but when I hit that stage – wherever it is – I'm at home again.

'Forever the most beautiful soul'
@GeorgeftParkerr

'It was a privilege though, wasn't it? To love him'
@mcguinessismine

'Tom was an amazing, beautiful and fiercely loving person. The endless positivity, light and joy he brought into this world will always be remembered. There are no words for how much we love and miss you, Tom. Thank you for everything'
@TheWantedUSFans

'Missing you so much Tommy, fly high angel'
@rebeccawalshol2

'Tom Parker's last gift to everyone was to bring the dudes back together so they could see how loved and missed they were. He is the light that'll never fade and will be absolutely missed'
@marlenvargas

'Rest in paradise Tommy P, love you so much, forever and always'
@thewantedmily

'Parts of Tom will always live on. He lives in each and every one of us and nobody will ever be able to take that from us. Our boy forever!'
@urtinyson

'The fact that Tom actually made it to tour to perform with his band and see his fans one last time, no matter how ill he was... He's a legend of his time'
@lucymaygoodwin

'Always my hero'
@itssgeOrgia

'Saddened to hear of the passing of the remarkable @tomparker. Sending sincere sympathy to @being_kelsey, Aurelia, Bodhi, his parents, brother, extended family, friends and his @thewanted brothers. Inspirational man who did so much good. May he Rest in Peace'
@Pollyt22

'What an absolute honour to spend our time in the presence of someone like Tom, there will never be another Tom'
@Clo_TheWantedx

'Tom will forever be my hero! A true fighter and we'll cherish the best moments'
@nicole_ly_tw

'I wish I had words. But I really don't. I'm so goddamn heartbroken for our TomTom, his beautiful family, our amazing boys and this one-of-a-kind fandom. I can't even begin to process this'
@hollypepper_tw

'I know I speak for everyone when I say I am beyond proud of his courage and fight up until the very last moment – Tom Parker you really were one in a million'
@stephxbraid

'Tom, your bravery has helped many. For that we are truly grateful. Your memory will live on. We'll make sure of it'
@JessTheWanted

'Our Tom Tom. Our superhero. A warrior always and forever and a true inspiration. Love you so much, Tommy P. Our hearts are shattered and will never heal but we will always remember you and share the complete joy you always brought us. Love you forever'
@_TWNostalgia

'My universe will never be the same'
@_megsconnolly

'How truly lucky are we, to know him, to love him, to
have the memories we have with him, they will never
make another person like him again! Our Tommy P,
forever and always'
@annataft_

'The brightest star in the sky. I love you forever Tommy P'
@holliebrown1

'I go to sleep tonight knowing heaven has gained an
angel! Watch over us all Tom, party hard tonight'
@EllieRiley_11

'The man with the most infectious smile, laugh and
personality. Heartbroken doesn't even come close.
Your memory will live on today and forever after that.
Thomas Parker, a true hero'
@tabitha_macknay

'Where do I start? Thank you. Thank you for the laughs
and the memories, thank you for giving me some of my
best friends and thank you for just being you. I'm so
thankful that somehow in life I got to know a person
like you and forever thankful I met you the times I did'
@chlo_nicole

'A smile so infectious it could light up the entire room, he truly was our hero and my heart aches. Fly high, Tom'
@omgbecs

'11-year-old me chose the best band. Will forever be proud of everything Tom has achieved. A true inspiration'
@eliseeeetw

'I don't have the words but all I can say is I'm so glad I finally got to see the boy back up on that stage where he belongs, one last time. Thank you for everything @TomParker'
@ParkersPeepsTW

'You did us proud til the very end Tom – fly high'
@beccaclaire92

'I can't actually believe it. Rest in peace Tommy, we love you more than you will ever know'
@beauticoleex

'Tom will forever be our hero. One of the strongest and bravest heroes I've ever known. We're so lucky to have watched him grow over the years, we really did choose the right man as our idol and hero. Tommy P in our hearts forever'
@Daisy_TW_JLS

'You led us with love and laughter, we promise
to do the same'
@CaroDolphin

'Tom was a legend and him being so positive all
the way through lifted my spirits and taught me to have
more strength. I'm devastated but still so incredibly
proud of Tom and I'm glad he got to do the tour.
He made me smile when I saw the boys and I hope
to have his strength'
@tw_egf

'We will always own the night in your memory as
we will continue to show the world how loved and
appreciated you forever will be. You will be sadly missed
but also remembered as the legend that you are.
We love you always'
@FOR3V3RF4NMAILY

'The relationships that Tom and the band have with
their fans is like no other. You were always made to
feel important. Like a friend. Tom always ALWAYS had
time for us. Tom wished us happy birthday, encouraged
us when going for jobs, congratulated us when we had
babies or got married #teamcougz'
@kimberleyw1983

'Rest in peace Tom Parker
Your home is now in heaven above;
So many people will feel an all time low at this sad news,
You are gone far too soon.
But, you will always be remembered with love.
We are so glad you came into our lives with The Wanted.
Death is a distance that parts broken hearts.
But, time brings us back together;
Your star will continue to flow in the dark
And be as bright as lightning chasing the sun,
You will always be missed
And the memories of you will be gold forever.
Sending love to your family, friends, your brothers in
the wanted and your fans.'
@allontheboard